W9-BYK-337

DISCARD

Sports and Athletes

Other Books of Related Interest:

Opposing Viewpoints Series

Girls and Sports

Education

Health

At Issue Series

Can Busy Teens Succeed Academically?

Can Celebrities Change the World?

The Olympics

The Rising Cost of College

"Congress shall make no law . . . abridging the freedom of speech, or of the press."

First Amendment to the U.S. Constitution

The basic foundation of our democracy is the First Amendment guarantee of freedom of expression. The Opposing Viewpoints Series is dedicated to the concept of this basic freedom and the idea that it is more important to practice it than to enshrine it.

OPPOSING VIEWPOINTS® SERIES

Sports and Athletes

Christine Watkins, Book Editor

GREENHAVEN PRESS
A part of Gale, Cengage Learning

GALE
CENGAGE Learning·

Detroit • New York • San Francisco • New Haven, Conn • Waterville, Maine • London

Christine Nasso, *Publisher*
Elizabeth Des Chenes, *Managing Editor*

© 2009 Greenhaven Press, a part of Gale, Cengage Learning.

Gale and Greenhaven Press are registered trademarks used herein under license.

For more information, contact:
Greenhaven Press
27500 Drake Rd.
Farmington Hills, MI 48331-3535
Or you can visit our Internet site at gale.cengage.com

For product information and technology assistance, contact us at

Gale Customer Support, 1-800-877-4253
For permission to use material from this text or product, submit all requests online at
www.cengage.com/permissions

Further permissions questions can be emailed to permissionrequest@cengage.com

Articles in Greenhaven Press anthologies are often edited for length to meet page require-ments. In addition, original titles of these works are changed to clearly present the main thesis and to explicitly indicate the author's opinion. Every effort is made to ensure that Greenhaven Press accurately reflects the original intent of the authors. Every effort has been made to trace the owners of copyrighted material.

Cover photograph © 2009 Jupiterimages.com.

LIBRARY OF CONGRESS CATALOGING-IN-PUBLICATION DATA

Sports and athletes / Christine Watkins, book editor.
    p. cm. -- (Opposing viewpoints)
    Includes bibliographical references and index.
    ISBN 978-0-7377-4542-9 (hardcover)
    ISBN 978-0-7377-4543-6 (pbk.)
    1. Sports--Juvenile literature. 2. Athletes--Juvenile literature. 3. Sports--Moral and ethical aspects--Juvenile literature. I. Watkins, Christine, 1951-
    GV705.4.S64 2009
    796--dc22
                                                                    2008045344

Printed in the United States of America
1 2 3 4 5 6 7 13 12 11 10 09

Contents

Chapter 3: Is There Equality in Sports?

Chapter 4: Is Drug Use a Problem in Sports?

Why Consider Opposing Viewpoints?

> *"The only way in which a human being can make some approach to knowing the whole of a subject is by hearing what can be said about it by persons of every variety of opinion and studying all modes in which it can be looked at by every character of mind. No wise man ever acquired his wisdom in any mode but this."*
>
> *John Stuart Mill*

In our media-intensive culture it is not difficult to find differing opinions. Thousands of newspapers and magazines and dozens of radio and television talk shows resound with differing points of view. The difficulty lies in deciding which opinion to agree with and which "experts" seem the most credible. The more inundated we become with differing opinions and claims, the more essential it is to hone critical reading and thinking skills to evaluate these ideas. Opposing Viewpoints books address this problem directly by presenting stimulating debates that can be used to enhance and teach these skills. The varied opinions contained in each book examine many different aspects of a single issue. While examining these conveniently edited opposing views, readers can develop critical thinking skills such as the ability to compare and contrast authors' credibility, facts, argumentation styles, use of persuasive techniques, and other stylistic tools. In short, the Opposing Viewpoints Series is an ideal way to attain the higher-level thinking and reading skills so essential in a culture of diverse and contradictory opinions.

In addition to providing a tool for critical thinking, Opposing Viewpoints books challenge readers to question their own strongly held opinions and assumptions. Most people form their opinions on the basis of upbringing, peer pressure, and personal, cultural, or professional bias. By reading carefully balanced opposing views, readers must directly confront new ideas as well as the opinions of those with whom they disagree. This is not to simplistically argue that everyone who reads opposing views will—or should—change his or her opinion. Instead, the series enhances readers' understanding of their own views by encouraging confrontation with opposing ideas. Careful examination of others' views can lead to the readers' understanding of the logical inconsistencies in their own opinions, perspective on why they hold an opinion, and the consideration of the possibility that their opinion requires further evaluation.

Evaluating Other Opinions

To ensure that this type of examination occurs, Opposing Viewpoints books present all types of opinions. Prominent spokespeople on different sides of each issue as well as well-known professionals from many disciplines challenge the reader. An additional goal of the series is to provide a forum for other, less known, or even unpopular viewpoints. The opinion of an ordinary person who has had to make the decision to cut off life support from a terminally ill relative, for example, may be just as valuable and provide just as much insight as a medical ethicist's professional opinion. The editors have two additional purposes in including these less known views. One, the editors encourage readers to respect others' opinions—even when not enhanced by professional credibility. It is only by reading or listening to and objectively evaluating others' ideas that one can determine whether they are worthy of consideration. Two, the inclusion of such viewpoints encourages the important critical thinking skill of objectively evaluating an author's credentials and bias. This evaluation will illuminate an author's reasons for taking a particular stance on an issue and will aid in readers' evaluation of the author's ideas.

It is our hope that these books will give readers a deeper understanding of the issues debated and an appreciation of the complexity of even seemingly simple issues when good and honest people disagree. This awareness is particularly important in a democratic society such as ours in which people enter into public debate to determine the common good. Those with whom one disagrees should not be regarded as enemies but rather as people whose views deserve careful examination and may shed light on one's own.

Thomas Jefferson once said that "difference of opinion leads to inquiry, and inquiry to truth." Jefferson, a broadly educated man, argued that "if a nation expects to be ignorant and free . . . it expects what never was and never will be." As individuals and as a nation, it is imperative that we consider the opinions of others and examine them with skill and discernment. The Opposing Viewpoints Series is intended to help readers achieve this goal.

David L. Bender and Bruno Leone,
Founders

Introduction

> *"Because sports participation can have such a positive impact on young people, it's extremely important that parents and coaches keep the games in perspective and the interests of the participants at the very top of the priority list."*
>
> *—Clark Kellogg,*
> *basketball analyst*
> *and former player in the*
> *National Basketball Association (NBA).*

It is widely accepted that playing sports benefits youth in many ways. Athletics can provide such positive and life-long lessons as goal-setting, perseverance, self-discipline, and teamwork. Playing sports also has been linked to improved academic and occupational outcomes, physical fitness, and enhanced self-esteem. However, in the past several years youth sports have also been producing symptoms of low self-esteem, depression, even panic attacks in many kids, and a tremendous drop-out rate in athletic participation, especially among twelve- to fourteen-year-olds. What is undermining the positive experience of sports for kids? Many experts believe the culprit is professionalization; the concept of winning at all costs is overriding fun, camaraderie, and sportsmanship. Dan Gould, director of the Michigan State University Institute for the Study of Youth Sports, explains: "Examples of this professional model include adults pressuring kids to win at early ages, along with single-sports specialization and year-round training at an early age."

Young athletes, as well as their parents, cannot help but take notice of the celebrity status given by the media and the public to star athletes. Many experts are concerned that the coverage of youth sports is becoming as excessive and comprehensive as that of college and professional sports. They point to Web sites that maintain current national rankings of middle and high school players and to colleges that send out scouts to recruit kids as young as fourteen years old. Overzealous parents, perhaps with dreams of college scholarships and million-dollar professional sports contracts, want to make sure their children are not left out of the limelight. So instead of allowing their kids time to enjoy unstructured play and to explore a variety of sports, such parents push their children to specialize at a young age in one sport, to train hard, and to play at the top level. "I have heard of instances in which parents delayed entering their children (especially boys) in kindergarten for a year, not because they judged that their children required a year to mature cognitively but rather so that they would be at a physical advantage in school sports," wrote self-esteem expert and motivational speaker Robert Brooks in his article "Some Thoughts About Youth Sports." Coaches also have reported that some parents actually pack up and move their families from one community to another so that their child can attend a particular high school—not for better educational opportunities, but to better showcase his or her athletic abilities. Additionally, parents spend thousands of dollars on personal trainers and private clinics, as well as on membership fees and travel expenses so that their children can play on elite club teams. The end result is that many young athletes are not playing for fun and recreation; they are playing to win—in large part because their parents have invested so much time and money. Child development experts and sports reformers maintain that the toll on these kids is tremendous.

Take for example an experience that high school varsity softball coach Jim Bennet described.

> "During a game, one of my best players struck out three
> times. I later learned that after the game was over and she
> went home, her parents made her take batting practice for

three hours—three hours that could have been spent doing homework, or eating with her family, or just sleeping. The next game she struck out again, so obviously the pressure from her parents didn't help. If it did anything, it made things worse. You could see it in the way she hung her head that she wasn't having any fun. Parents are so hard on them. It's crazy."

In addition to the emotional strain on young athletes, sports-related injuries are escalating. Because many kids are playing only one sport and competing year-round, they are especially susceptible to repetitive stress or overuse injuries. Without downtime and rest, tendons and bones get worn down from repetitious motion. Dr. Ronald Kamm, director of Sport Psychiatry Associates in Oakhurst, New Jersey, told Regan McMahon for her book *Revolution in the Bleachers: How Parents Can Take Back Family Life in a World Gone Crazy Over Youth Sports*, "We enacted child labor laws eighty years ago to protect children from all this work. And now basically we're making play into work. And they're working as hard as they used to in the sweat shops, some of them. I'm concerned about it; it's out of hand, and kids do need downtime and seasons off and multiple sports."

Looking on the bright side, however, more and more people are recognizing today's professionalization of youth sports and the win-at-all-cost mentality, and they are working diligently to make changes. For example, Jim Thompson founded the Positive Coaching Alliance (PCA) to promote the beneficial and fun aspects of sports. He has created workshops for coaches and parents, and some county leagues have made attendance at these workshops mandatory. Furthermore, many sports medicine specialists, child psychologists, and sports reformers are speaking out about the importance of physical and emotional balance in children's lives—and parents and coaches are listening. In *The Oregonian*, high school football coach Tom Smythe expressed his views against summer football camps: "For crying out loud, football at the high school level is supposed to be fun. . . . How about giving the kids some family time? Maybe let them have some freedom to go with their girlfriends to the beach. Or maybe just to lounge around and do nothing. Isn't that what summers are for?"

The professionalism of youth sports is only one of many components that make up today's sports culture. Other controversies include athletes as role models, equality in sports, and the use of performance-enhancing drugs. *Opposing Viewpoints: Sports and Athletes* examines society's attitudes about sports in the following chapters: Do Sports Benefit Children? Should College Sports Be Reformed? Is There Equality in Sports? Is Drug Use a Problem in Sports? In these chapters, the authors discuss the role of sports in society and debate what, if any, reforms should be undertaken.

OPPOSING
VIEWPOINTS®
SERIES

CHAPTER 1

Do Sports Benefit Children?

Chapter Preface

Playing sports can change lives—often for the better. Take, for example, the life of Elliot Taylor. As a sophomore in high school, Taylor was propelling toward a dead-end future. "I was lost. I was doing all kinds of things, like gangs and stuff," Taylor explained. "A typical day for me was to go to the store, steal something, and then hang around with my gangster friends on the corner. I had no direction. I didn't know where I was going." Then the football coaches at a San Diego, California, high school brought him into their fold; as a result, Elliot Taylor made the honor roll the next two years and graduated from high school in 2008 with hopes of attending college. Taylor's English teacher told the *San Diego Union-Tribune*'s Bill Dickens, "When he first came to school here, I couldn't reach him. Then he got attracted to sports. He's become extremely self-motivated with goals and a positive look at the future."

Throughout the United States, many organizations are reaching out to young people like Elliot Taylor who otherwise would not get involved with organized sports, and thus miss out on the many important life skills associated with sports participation. The First Tee Life Skills Experience was developed in Detroit, Michigan, to help kids aged five through eighteen learn the game of golf. Joe Louis Barrow Jr., chief executive officer of The First Tee, explains, "By participating in a non-threatening, non-instructive environment, kids typically learn to set goals, control emotions, and resolve conflicts while learning a game that can be played for a lifetime." To reach the inner-city middle school students in San Francisco, California, Johanna Thomashefski helped establish Lacrosse for Life. Thomashefski believes that participants will learn to play the game of lacrosse and at the same time gain a sense of achievement, responsibility for their own actions, and respect—for themselves and for those in authority. And Nashville RBI provides the inner-city youth in Nashville, Tennessee, with opportunities to play baseball and softball while inspiring them to recognize their potential, encouraging academic excellence, and increasing their self-esteem, all while having fun.

Athletic programs that teach positive ideals along with the sport can have a life-changing impact on youth—particularly on troubled and disadvantaged youth—just as the football program did for Elliot Taylor. Such children, according to experts in child development and social services, often come from unstable single-parent homes that lack structure and supervision; many of these kids feel abandoned by adults and have few positive role models. Programs such as The First Tee, Lacrosse for Life, and Nashville RBI appear to be effective in filling the gaps in the lives of these underserved youth and in bolstering their feelings of value and self-worth. And the programs are producing their own positive returns. In an article by Marcia Bradford, "Changing Lives: How Sports Planners Are Impacting Youth for Life," Joe Louis Barrow Jr. of The First Tee said, "Recently a young woman, about fifteen, from the Atlanta area, returned to the program to help out some of the younger participants. She expressed concern for them and said she wanted to make sure they didn't make the same mistakes she did when she was their age. It was clear that she had become a mentor."

The gains from participating in sports are numerous, from increased physical fitness to positive self-esteem and even economic success. But there also are inherent risks. In the following chapter, the authors discuss the pros and cons of sports participation for children.

> *"Other things being equal, if a kid plays sports, he will earn more money, stay in school longer, and be more engaged in civic life."*

Sports Benefit Children

Scott Ganz and Kevin Hassett

In the following viewpoint, Scott Ganz and Kevin Hassett contend that athletes achieve a higher level of education, earn higher wages, and become more civic-minded than non-athletes. Ganz and Hassett believe that these life-long advantages result from the emotional attachment to competition and the intense desire to win that many athletes develop through participation in sports. Scott Ganz is a research assistant at the American Enterprise Institute, and Kevin Hassett is the American Enterprise Institute's director of economic policy studies.

As you read, consider the following questions:

1. According to research studies, do students involved in such activities as band, student government, or theater become as successful in life as athletes?

2. Do the authors believe that part of a coach's job is to teach a child to care about winning?

3. Has research found that most Americans think success in life is largely determined by luck or through hard work?

When pundits discuss the influence of sports on American culture, they often emphasize the negatives: [professional football quarterback] Michael Vick and dogfighting; the steroids scandals in baseball; lewd fan behavior in football; doping incidents in cycling and track. But below the radar of popular athletic culture is something that has profoundly shaped the lives of millions of Americans for the better: youth sports. A growing body of research is showing the social and economic benefits of participation in youth sports to be surprisingly large and overwhelmingly positive. Other things being equal, if a kid plays sports, he will earn more money, stay in school longer, and be more engaged in civic life.

Turning Rebellion into Discipline

To understand how and why this might be so, consider the case of Sandy Brown, who works with the Positive Coaching Alliance (PCA), a national nonprofit organization that aims to improve the quality of youth coaching in America. As a youngster, Brown was frequently in trouble and had been kicked out of school for fighting and other unruly behavior. But Brown's life was turned around by a grade school principal and football coach named Bill Spencer. According to the PCA website, Spencer confronted his difficult new student one day and said, "Brown, I know what your problem is." Sandy thought he knew what was coming next, because he had heard this speech so many times before: "*You're no good; you'll never amount to anything.*" But Spencer saw something else in the young man— potential. "Brown, you get into fights all the time because you want to compete. You have the heart of a winner."

Brown went on to play football for Spencer and had an impressive career. He is now a legendary coach at the Giddings State School, a youth detention facility in Giddings, Texas. Brown molds groups of violent young offenders into disciplined and winning football teams. Having won three state championships in the second-largest classification of the Texas Association of Private and Parochial Schools, he is regularly recruited by other "normal" schools, but feels his job at Giddings is too rewarding to relinquish.

Brown takes kids who have committed heinous crimes and gives them hope. And he does that by making the game a metaphor for life. In a speech he delivered to his players in 1997 that was recounted in a *Sports Illustrated* profile, Brown said,

> "You boys had some tough breaks in life. You had judges who locked you up. You had parents who kicked your behinds and didn't give you the love you wanted. But let me tell you something: What happens to you tonight is up to you. You're the only ones out here who can change yourselves for the better. . . . You've got to stand up. Do you hear me? You've got to stand up and be a man, or bow your head and be a loser."

Providing Advantages over Non-Athletes

Feel-good stories such as this help illustrate a larger point. An increasing quantity of research suggests that people like Spencer, Brown, and other youth coaches have a major impact on the lives of their charges. One study, by economists John M. Barron and Glen R. Waddell of Purdue University and Bradley T. Ewing of Texas Tech University, examines a series of surveys taken by American males who attended high school in the 1970s. It found that high school athletes achieved a level of education 25 to 35 percent higher than their non-athlete classmates.

It's not just educational achievement that correlates with youth-sports participation. Barron, Waddell, and Ewing also found that high school athletes had 12 to 31 percent higher wages than their non-athlete counterparts. And when the wages of college graduates who were high school athletes are compared with those who were not, the athletes generally made higher wages—on average, $73 more per week. It's pretty clear that athletes win in the workplace, too.

Athletics also seems to give a bigger edge to students than other activities, such as band, student government, or theater. In another paper, Ewing estimates that, all else equal, athletes earn roughly 6 percent more than non-athletes, translating into around $1,000 per year extra wages.

Of course, it's possible that participation in athletics is just a proxy for other talents and abilities. Maybe sports do not really have a beneficent effect at the margin; perhaps it's just that more able people tend to participate in sports.

To investigate this possibility, Barron, Waddell, and Ewing also control for a number of variables in order to see if athletes are higher achievers because they share some other common characteristic. The authors examine IQ test results and standardized test scores and find that an "athlete premium" remains even after controlling for intelligence. In other words, if you take two kids who have the same IQ and put one in a sports program, he will have a better future.

Athletes are also more active citizens, a 2006 study found. Economists Mark Hugo Lopez and Kimberlee Moore of the University of Maryland examined the effect of participation in sports on civic engagement. After controlling for factors such as age, educational attainment, and income, they found that athletes are 15 percent more likely to be registered to vote, 14 percent more likely to watch the news, and 8 percent more likely to feel comfortable speaking in public (and, for public speaking, the effect on females is twice as large).

Producing a Desire to Excel

Why would participation in sports be associated with many benefits? Distinguished sports historian Allen Guttmann pro-

The Champions' Trophy: What Makes Athletes Elite

Confident

Self-motivated

Strong character

Ability to be criticized

Never-quit attitude

Aggressive

Focused

Understand time management

Deal well with pressure

Learn from mistakes

Welcome challenge

Make sacrifices

Team oriented

Accountable

Disciplined

Coachable

Committed

Competitive

Goal oriented

Overcome adversity

Tremendous work ethic

Mental / physical toughness

THE CHAMPIONS' TROPHY

Athletes 4 Hire,
"Champions' Trophy: What Makes Collegiate Athletes Elite?"
Athletes4Hire.com, 2006.

vides a clue. He notes that ancient sports were highly religious affairs, and competition was organized in order to please the gods. Modern sports, however, have an entirely different character. Guttmann comments, "Once the gods have vanished from Mount Olympus or from Dante's paradise, we can no longer run to appease them or to save our souls, but we can set a new record. It is a uniquely modern form of immortality."

Small tastes of that immortality are available to today's athletes at many levels. Indeed, we speak from personal experience. What we have learned coaching youth baseball suggests why sports, especially modern team sports, can be so transformative.

For starters, one thing we have noticed is that no matter how low the stakes, the participants' emotional attachment to competition is intense. There seems to be little distinguishable difference between the transcendent joy of a World Series victor and a local Little League champion. A kid who has never had a hit in his life will feel like a Major League all-star when he rounds first base after his first line-drive up the middle. It's doubtful there is a former Little Leaguer around who doesn't rate his first home run as one of the happiest moments of his childhood.

A coach does not have to teach a kid to care about winning. Indeed, the problem is the reverse. The youth coach's role is to focus on sportsmanship, effort, and excellence precisely because the obsession over the outcome is so innate and so strong.

But since individuals care so much about the outcome, they experience—perhaps in a way that is unprecedented in a young life—a desire for excellence. Once this fire is lit, the change in the behavior of kids on a team can be extraordinary. Parents do not have to hound kids to practice. They do so voluntarily. And when they do, they almost always improve.

The positive feedback between effort and results can then lead to snowballing commitments to excellence. One particularly successful cohort in our league, for example, consisted of kids who would organize informal practices at the local ball field. If you drove past the park on the way home from work, the odds were pretty good that half a dozen 12-year-olds would be on the diamond, working out.

Teaching a Formula for Success

This lesson—that hard work can lead to excellence—is one that can transform lives. Almost all of life in a capitalist society involves some form of competition. Young athletes learn the formula for success in a market-based system. And the evidence says they outperform their peers throughout their lifetimes.

A recent scholarly paper by economists Alberto Alesina and Edward Glaeser of Harvard University and Bruce Sacerdote of Dartmouth College found that countries tend to build large welfare states when citizens believe that success in life is largely determined by luck. When citizens believe that hard work determines success, they tend to build leaner and more economically efficient governments.

Americans are remarkably different from Europeans in this regard. If you ask Americans whether the economically disadvantaged are poor because they are lazy or unlucky, 60 percent say lazy. If you ask Europeans, only 26 percent finger laziness. Alesina and his colleagues argue that these attitudes shape society by shaping governmental and social institutions.

But why do these attitudes exist? A big part of the answer may be found in sports. A 1999 study by developmental psychologists Françoise D. Alsaker and August Flammer found American children spend more time participating in athletics than Europeans. In certain cases—America compared with France, for instance—the gap is quite substantial. A 1996 study by Michigan State University sports psychologist Martha

E. Ewing and Vern D. Seefeldt, former director of the Institute for the Study of Youth Sports, found that 45 percent of all eligible American youths play in an agency-sponsored league, like Little League baseball or Pop Warner football. That is 22 million children each year who get an infusion of the American work ethos.

Americans learn on the ball field or in the gym that effort and success are connected. Convinced that effort matters, we extend more effort, and celebrate and protect the fruits of effort.

Why have Americans been unwilling to build a European welfare state? Because they believe that income differences are largely attributable to effort difference. Why do they believe that effort matters? Maybe it's because they play Little League.

> "*It's ironic that sports, an endeavor meant to be, at its core, healthy exercise, is in fact hurtful to kids if they are training too hard and constantly.*"

Sports Can Harm Children Who Train Too Vigorously

National Alliance for Youth Sports

An increasing number of young athletes are experiencing bone fractures and other serious injuries, according to the National Alliance for Youth Sports (NAYS). In the following viewpoint, the authors argue that kids today tend to specialize in one sport with year-round practice and game schedules, creating constant stress on their young developing bodies. As a result, overuse injuries involving tissue, muscles, and bones are emerging as a disturbing trend. The National Alliance for Youth Sports, a nonprofit organization, advocates for positive and safe sports and activities for children.

As you read, consider the following questions:

1. What are two factors that contribute to the rise in overuse injuries among young athletes, according to the National Alliance for Youth Sports?

National Alliance for Youth Sports, "Overdoing It," NAYS.org, May 6, 2008. Reproduced by permission.

2. The Tommy John ligament surgery is performed to repair what kind of sports injury?

3. According to the authors, how has Little League International modified the rule on pitching restrictions?

In today's age of sports specialization, heavy practice schedules and year-round training, a disturbing number of young athletes are having their seasons chopped short—and their long-term health jeopardized—by overuse injuries.

As more and more youngsters are forced to visit doctor's offices for everything from bone fractures and Little League elbow to shin splints and damaged knees, the alarm is being sounded loud and clear by sports medicine professionals that too much of the same activity can do more harm than good.

Overdoing It

Overuse injuries are sabotaging what should be a fun and rewarding experience for millions of young athletes. These children, who are breaking down due to the constant stress being placed on their young and developing bodies, often face the unenviable prospect of long and sometimes painful rehabilitations, and even surgery, to repair the damage.

"What people need to know is that children are not young adults when it comes to their bodies and sports," says Dr. John DiFiori, professor and chief of the Division of Sports Medicine at UCLA and team physician for the UCLA Department of Intercollegiate Athletics. "We see a variety of different types of problems in our offices involving tissue, muscles and bones."

Overuse injuries have emerged as a disturbing trend fueled by several factors: Kids specializing in one sport before puberty; parents blinded by the pursuit of athletic scholarships pushing their children beyond what is acceptable; youngsters participating on travel teams or playing on multiple teams during the same season; negligent coaches pushing youngsters beyond what is acceptable just to win another game; and young athletes simply not giving their bodies any rest between seasons.

"Overuse injuries are extremely common in youth sports," says Dr. Johnny Benjamin, chairman of the Department of Orthopedic Surgery at the Indian River Medical Center in Vero Beach, Fla. "The dynamics of youth sports have changed over the years. No longer does a talented athlete play all sports and move from one sport to another as the seasons change. Now these child athletes are forced to specialize in a single sport year round and they participate on multiple teams in multiple leagues, many times simultaneously."

The American Academy of Pediatrics estimates that more than 30 million children and teens participate in organized sports each year. Of those, approximately 3.5 million seek treatment for overuse injuries and chronic fatigue from over-training.

While specific data doesn't exist regarding the number of overuse injuries occurring in youth sports, there is little debate among the sports medicine community that they are on the rise.

Focusing on a Single Sport

"We do know that there are approximately 30 million children involved in some form of youth sports," says DiFiori. "We also know more and more of these kids are participating on nearly a year-round basis and in some cases, without question, more of them are participating in a single sport at a young age. In the past some might play a particular sport in the fall and something different in the winter, but now some kids are participating in the same activity in different forms year round. We know the kinds of things that will contribute to the development of overuse injuries and we're seeing them in our office, no question about that."

Since the advent of organized youth sports, sitting on the bench while teammates played has never been a lot of fun for children. Yet nowadays, that is where many youngsters find themselves when their bodies simply aren't developed enough to withstand the wear and tear of a heavy load of games, practices, specialty camps and the never-ending training sessions that they go through.

"The dramatic rise in overuse injuries among children is particularly heartbreaking considering what the doctors told me: That overuse injuries are preventable," says Regan McMahon, a *San Francisco Chronicle* reporter who spoke with countless experts in the field while authoring her book *Revolution in the Bleachers*. "The only conclusion to draw from this is that kids are being hurt unnecessarily. It's ironic that sports, an endeavor meant to be, at its core, healthy exercise, is in fact hurtful to kids if they are training too hard and constantly."

The Tommy John ligament surgery, an elbow procedure named after the former Los Angeles Dodgers pitcher who was the first to have it done, used to be performed on pitchers in their 20s—but not any longer. Since the pitching motion is an unnatural one—and with a child throwing too many of them coupled with inadequate rest—it's not uncommon for kids who haven't even reached their teenage years to have this surgery done to repair their arms.

Dr. James Andrews, the nationally renowned orthopedic surgeon, says that he is seeing four times as many overuse injuries in youth sports than just five years ago, and that more kids are having surgery for chronic sports injuries, too.

Dr. John Moor, the orthopedic surgeon for the Cincinnati Reds, told the *Sarasota Herald-Tribune*: "Unless we do things differently, we're giving these kids life-altering injuries. We're taking away their ability, as they become adults, to really enjoy the full extent and range of their bodies."

Raising Awareness

Sometimes overuse injuries can be attributed to parents and coaches putting pressure on the child to excel simply to attain athletic glory, regardless of the health risks.

"Parents, coaches and the commercialization of athletics in general are unfortunately the culprits," Benjamin says. "The potential perfect storm occurs when a demanding parent, with possibly unrealized personal aspirations, an aggressive coach with their sights set on advancing to the next level and pay for play models—such as traveling teams, sports academies, personal position coaches and clinics—meet."

Other times, it can be the case of a self-driven youngster simply pushing himself to be the best he can be, unaware of the physical limitations of his young body. Clearly, a fine line exists between children being dedicated to a sport and forcing themselves to do too much.

"As healthcare educators in sports medicine, we attempt to raise awareness constantly," says Dr. Jeff Konin, executive director of the Sports Medicine & Athletic Related Trauma (SMART) Institute at the University of South Florida. "The attitude of 'it won't happen to me' is prevalent, and the drive to win and compete is contagious, many times being pushed by parents and coaches. Perhaps more public figures speaking out would help, but for them to do so potentially admits fault on their part or their medical team, thus you won't see this often. Perhaps technological education campaigns would be more effective than current print media, such as podcasts or injuries integrated into computer games."

Some of the major players in youth sports are beginning to take significant steps to address the epidemic. Little League International recently modified its decades-old rules on pitching restrictions. Rather than placing a limit on the number of innings that a child can pitch per week, restrictions are now based on the number of pitches actually thrown. While the switch is definitely a step in the right direction, it does little to address the ones most in danger—youth athletes who play on multiple teams, year-round.

"Limiting pitch counts per game and week—versus previous rules of limiting innings thrown—has certainly assisted with the potential reduction of elbow and shoulder injuries, though no proof actually exists to date," Konin says. "However, outside of a single league that a child plays in, these rules are extremely stretched. For example, no rules exist for limitations of throwing during practice, and no rule exists that limits a child to playing on one team, so many kids who take the sport seriously play in more than one league, where 'interleague monitoring' does not exist."

Coaching Counts

Modifying rules in youth sports, like pitching restrictions, will hopefully contribute to alleviating the problem of overuse injuries. But rather than relying on youth sports organizations like Little League to mandate change, coaches can do their part, too. By proactively preventing such unnecessary injuries by making sure that their players are receiving adequate rest, nutrition and are using proper form and technique, many problems can be avoided.

Sometimes, injuries thought to be related to overuse are actually the result of poor mechanics. Teaching young athletes the proper technique for a particular sports skill is not done solely to increase performance, but also to prevent injury. Overuse injuries can sometimes be prevented by using movements that are less taxing on specific body parts.

Although some experts often differentiate overuse-related injuries from injuries caused by improper form, using proper form can decrease the chances of an overuse injury occurring. That is why it is incumbent upon youth sports coaches to not only monitor how often their players are performing a particular skill, but also in what manner they are executing it.

Types of Injuries Among Young Athletes

Acute Injuries

Acute injuries are caused by a sudden trauma. Common acute injuries among young athletes include contusions (bruises), sprains (a partial or complete tear of a ligament), strains (a partial or complete tear of a muscle or tendon), and fractures.

Overuse Injuries

Not all injuries are caused by a single, sudden twist, fall, or collision. A series of small injuries to an immature body can cause minor fractures, minimal muscle tears, or progressive bone deformities, known as overuse injuries.

An example of an overuse injury is "Little League Elbow." This is the term used to describe a group of common overuse injuries in young throwers involved in many sports, not just baseball. Other common overuse injuries can tear the tendons in heels and knees.

Contact Sports Injuries

Contact sports have inherent dangers that put young athletes at special risk for severe injuries. Even with rigorous training and proper safety equipment, children are at risk for severe injuries to the neck, spinal cord, and growth plates. Following the rules of the game and using proper equipment can decrease these risks.

American Academy of Orthopaedic Surgeons, "A Guide to Safety for Young Athletes," AAOS.org, October 2007.

"If mechanics are off, injury will likely occur and if injury occurs from normal biomechanics, then compensatory motions will lead to other injuries," says Konin in reference to the human body's natural inclination when injured to rely on non-injured body parts to compensate. For example, if a quarterback attempts to throw a ball while suffering from a leg injury, he will likely attempt to use more arm strength to compensate for the lack of leg strength—thus heightening the chance for an arm injury. Athletes at every level usually are not too anxious to come out of a game, which is why it is the coach's responsibility to make sure that a child never plays through an injury.

"If you have weak stomach muscles you will overuse the arm," says Michelle Cappello, sports medicine management coordinator for the Children's Hospital & Research Center in Oakland, Calif. "Sixty percent of the power when throwing comes from the torso and legs."

Preventing Injuries

Although all sports medicine experts agree that too much volume in any sport is never a good idea, many like Cappello also feel that a lot of today's overuse injuries can still be prevented with the use of safe and proper techniques.

Cappello oversees the Sports Medicine Center for Young Athletes, a program designed to offer young athletes, coaches, administrators and parents a resource for sports injury care and prevention or, as she describes it, "wellness education." The program addresses the problem of overuse injuries by proactively teaching proper technique and conditioning methods.

"We have an on-site lecture series for parents, coaches and athletes. We come in and talk about things like swimmers shoulder and ACL injury prevention," she says. "We can treat these things, but 50 percent of sports-related injuries are completely preventable, although you can make an argument that 100 percent are preventable."

Some of their seminars are centered on general sports movements, while others like "Tough Cuff" are designed to teach coaches and athletes proper strength and conditioning methods for the rotator cuff. They say that by training all muscle groups involved in the movement patterns of throwing an athlete can severely minimize the risk of injury.

While Cappello is confident that a significant portion of overuse injuries can be avoided with proper education on conditioning and technique, she still warns against overworking a child too much.

"The foundation that we build with these kids is really important with regard to how they perform movement," she says. "If you can really get the techniques down correctly they'll strengthen, but also, do they have enough rest built in? You have to look at the volume of exercise that these kids are doing. There is a point where too much volume is too much volume, but there are a lot of variables to it."

"Some girls who play sports or exercise intensely are at risk for a problem called female athlete triad."

Some Female Athletes Develop Unhealthy Practices

TeensHealth

The authors in the following viewpoint explain how some girls who train hard to be strong athletes may actually be putting their health at serious risk. According to the TeensHealth organization, when athletes do not balance sufficient nutrition with their intense training, they can develop symptoms of the Female Athlete Triad, a disorder that is a combination of three conditions: disordered eating, amenorrhea, and osteoporosis. Created by The Nemours Foundation's Center for Children's Health Media, the Web site TeensHealth and its related site, KidsHealth, provide teens and families with accurate health information.

As you read, consider the following questions:

1. According to the authors, is the eating disorder bulimia nervosa associated with the Female Athlete Triad?

2. When a girl's weight falls too low, how is her menstrual cycle affected?

3. Generally speaking, does losing weight improve athletic performance, according to the TeensHealth organization?

With dreams of college scholarships in her mind, Hannah joined the track team her freshman year and trained hard to become a lean, strong sprinter. When her coach told her losing a few pounds would improve her performance, she immediately started counting calories and increased the duration of her workouts. She was too busy with practices and meets to notice that her period had stopped—she was more worried about the stress fracture in her ankle slowing her down.

Although Hannah thinks her intense training and disciplined diet are helping her performance, they may actually be hurting her—and her health.

What Is Female Athlete Triad?

Sports and exercise are part of a balanced, healthy lifestyle. Girls who play sports are healthier; get better grades; are less likely to experience depression; and use alcohol, cigarettes, and drugs less frequently than girls who aren't athletes. But for some girls, not balancing the needs of their bodies and their sports can have major consequences.

Some girls who play sports or exercise intensely are at risk for a problem called female athlete triad. Female athlete triad is a combination of three conditions: disordered eating, amenorrhea, and osteoporosis. A female athlete can have one, two, or all three parts of the triad.

Triad Factor #1: Disordered Eating. Most girls with female athlete triad try to lose weight primarily to improve their athletic performance. The disordered eating that accompanies female athlete triad can range from avoiding certain types of food the athlete thinks are "bad" (such as foods containing fat) to serious eating disorders like anorexia nervosa or bulimia nervosa.

Triad Factor #2: Amenorrhea. Because a girl with female athlete triad is simultaneously exercising intensely and not eating enough calories, when her weight falls too low, she may experience decreases in estrogen, the hormone that helps to regulate the menstrual cycle. As a result, a girl's periods may become irregular or stop altogether. Of course, it is normal for teen girls to occasionally miss periods, especially in their first year of having periods. A missed period does not automatically mean a girl has female athlete triad. A missed period could mean something else is going on, like pregnancy or a medical condition. If you have missed a period and you are sexually active, talk to your doctor.

Some girls who participate intensively in sports may never even get their first period because they've been training so hard. Other girls may have had periods, but once they increase their training and change their eating habits, their periods may stop.

Triad Factor #3: Osteoporosis. Low estrogen levels and poor nutrition, especially low calcium intake, can lead to osteoporosis, the third aspect of the triad. Osteoporosis is a weakening of the bones due to the loss of bone density and improper bone formation. This condition can ruin a female athlete's career because it may lead to stress fractures and other injuries.

Usually, the teen years are a time when girls should be building up their bone mass to their highest levels—called peak bone mass. Not getting enough calcium during the teen years can also have a lasting effect on how strong a girl's bones are later in life.

Who Gets Female Athlete Triad?

Most girls have concerns about the size and shape of their bodies, but girls who develop female athlete triad have certain risk factors that set them apart. Being a highly competitive athlete and participating in a sport that requires you to train extra hard is a risk factor.

Girls with female athlete triad often care so much about their sports that they would do almost anything to improve their performance. Martial arts and rowing are examples of sports that classify athletes by weight class, so focusing on weight becomes an important part of the training program and can put a girl at risk for disordered eating.

Participation in sports where a thin appearance is valued can also put a girl at risk for female athlete triad. Sports such as gymnastics, figure skating, diving, and ballet are examples of sports that value a thin, lean body shape. Some girls may even be told by coaches or judges that losing weight would improve their scores.

Even in sports where body size and shape aren't as important, such as distance running and cross-country skiing, girls may be pressured by teammates, parents, partners, and coaches who mistakenly believe that "losing just a few pounds" could improve their performance.

The truth is, though, that losing those few pounds generally doesn't improve performance at all. People who are fit and active enough to compete in sports generally have more muscle than fat, so it's the muscle that gets starved when a girl cuts back on food. Plus, if a girl loses weight when she doesn't need to, it interferes with healthy body processes such as menstruation and bone development.

In addition, for some competitive female athletes, problems such as low self-esteem, a tendency toward perfectionism, and family stress place them at risk for disordered eating. . . .

How Can Doctors Help?

An extensive physical examination is a crucial part of diagnosing female athlete triad. A doctor who thinks a girl has female athlete triad will probably ask questions about her periods,

The Signs and Symptoms of Female Athlete Triad

Girls with female athlete triad often have signs and symptoms of eating disorders, such as:

- continued dieting in spite of weight loss

- preoccupation with food and weight

- frequent trips to the bathroom during and after meals

- using laxatives

- brittle hair or nails

- dental cavities because in girls with bulimia tooth enamel is worn away by frequent vomiting

- sensitivity to cold

- low heart rate and blood pressure

- heart irregularities and chest pain

TeensHealth, "Female Athlete Triad,"
TeensHealth.org, October 2006.

her nutrition and exercise habits, any medications she takes, and her feelings about her body. This is called the medical history.

Poor nutrition can also affect the body in many ways, so a doctor might order blood tests to check for anemia and other problems associated with the triad. The doctor also will check for medical reasons why a girl may be losing weight and missing her periods. Because osteoporosis can put a girl at higher risk for bone fractures, the doctor may also request tests to measure bone density.

Doctors don't work alone to help a girl with female athlete triad. Coaches, parents, physical therapists, pediatricians and adolescent medicine specialists, nutritionists and dietitians, and mental health specialists can all work together to treat the physical and emotional problems that a girl with female athlete triad faces.

It might be tempting for a girl with female athlete triad to shrug off several months of missed periods, but getting help right away is important. In the short term, she may have muscle weakness, stress fractures, and reduced physical performance. Over the long term, she may suffer from bone weakness, long-term effects on her reproductive system, and heart problems.

A girl who is recovering from female athlete triad may work with a dietitian to help get to and maintain a healthy weight and ensure she's eating enough calories and nutrients for health and good athletic performance. Depending on how much the girl is exercising, she may have to reduce the length of her workouts. Talking to a psychologist or therapist can help a girl deal with depression, pressure from coaches or family members, or low self-esteem and can help her find ways to deal with her problems other than restricting her food intake or exercising excessively.

Some girls with female athlete triad may need to take hormones to supply their bodies with estrogen so they can get their periods started again. In such cases, birth control pills are often used to regulate the menstrual cycle. Calcium and vitamin D supplementation is also common for a girl who has suffered bone loss as the result of female athlete triad.

What to Do if a Friend Has Symptoms

A girl with female athlete triad may try to hide it, but she can't just ignore the disorder and hope it goes away. She needs to get help from a doctor and other health professionals. If a friend, sister, or teammate has signs and symptoms of female athlete triad, discuss your concerns with her and encourage her to seek treatment. If she refuses to seek treatment, you may need to mention your concern to a parent, coach, teacher, or school nurse.

You may worry about being nosy when you ask questions about a friend's health, but you're not: Your concern is a sign that you're a caring friend. Lending an ear may be just what your friend needs.

How Can Female Athlete Triad Be Prevented?

Here are a few tips to help teen athletes stay on top of their physical condition:

- Keep track of your periods. It's easy to forget when you had your last visit from Aunt Flo, so keep a calendar in your gym bag and mark down when your period starts and stops and if the bleeding is particularly heavy or light. That way, if you start missing periods, you'll know right away and you'll have accurate information to give to your doctor.

- Don't skip meals or snacks. Girls who are constantly on the go between school, practice, and competitions may be tempted to skip meals and snacks to save time. But eating now will improve performance later, so stock your locker or bag with quick and easy favorites such as bagels, string cheese, unsalted nuts and seeds, raw vegetables, granola bars, and fruit.

- Visit a dietitian or nutritionist who works with teen athletes. He or she can help you get your dietary game plan into gear and determine if you're getting enough key nutrients such as iron, calcium, and protein. And if you need supplements, a nutritionist can recommend the best choices.

- Do it for you. Pressure from teammates, parents, or coaches can turn a fun activity into a nightmare. If you're not enjoying your sport, make a change. Remember: It's your body and your life. You—not your coach or teammates—will have to live with any damage you do to your body now.

> *"People in positions of influence, from parents to teachers to ministers to athletes and entertainers, need to be good role models and do what they can to influence our children to make the right decisions."*

Professional Athletes Should Be Role Models

Christian Malone

Christian Malone, a columnist for The Valdosta Daily Times *in Georgia, contends in the following viewpoint that professional athletes should be role models. According to Malone, many kids idolize athletes and consider them to be superstars; these athletes should recognize their positions of influence and act accordingly. He further maintains that because fans pay a lot of money to support athletes, the athletes should in turn support the fans by setting positive examples.*

As you read, consider the following questions:

1. Besides athletes, who else is in such influential positions to be considered role models, according to Christian Malone?

2. Why does the author believe former football star Danny Wuerffel is a good role model?

3. Why does the author believe that men such as Michael Vick and Pacman Jones should change their behavior?

The President of the United States [George W. Bush] thinks athletes and entertainers should be role models. I couldn't agree more.

Athletes and entertainers absolutely should be role models. Few people have more young boys and girls looking up to them. Their actions and words can make a positive impact on thousands of kids—or a negative one.

"People in the entertainment and sports industries serve as role models to millions of young Americans, and that comes with the responsibility to dispel the notion that drug abuse is glamorous and free of consequences," George W. Bush said during his weekly radio address.

Bush's comments were primarily about drug use, in light of all the attention the Mitchell Report [a report, released on December 13, 2007, to the commissioner of baseball about the illegal use of performance-enhancing drugs by major league baseball players] has received, and the way baseball players like Barry Bonds, Rogers Clemens and Andy Pettitte have used them to become better players. Bush has long been critical of the use of steroids and other performance-enhancing drugs, and understandably so. They have no place in baseball, and I hope the game eventually finds a way to eliminate them.

Athletes Hold Positions of Influence

But athletes, and other entertainers, should be role models in every sense of the word. They should set a positive example for others. They should stay out of trouble, and out of the police reports. They should work hard, and give their best to help their teams win. They should be drug-free. They should set an example for their young fans.

Most People Agree that Athletes Are Role Models For Children

Whether they like it or not, professional athletes are role models for children.

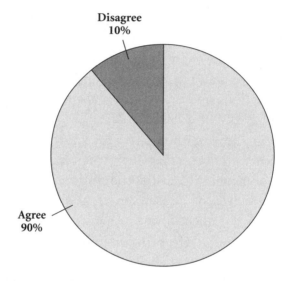

Disagree
10%

Agree
90%

TAKEN FROM: SI.com, "Homosexuality and Sports," posted April 12, 2005.

Athletes get paid large sums of money by their teams, and sometimes even larger sums by companies to endorse their products. Fans pay a good amount of money to watch these athletes play in person, too.

The least those athletes can do is set a positive example for others to follow.

People in positions of influence, from parents to teachers to ministers to athletes and entertainers, need to be good role models and do what they can to influence our children to make the right decisions. That means staying out of trouble and doing the right thing.

That means being someone we can root for as fans. That means being someone we can encourage our children to root for.

Many of our professional athletes are good role models, but unfortunately, they get overshadowed by those who aren't.

[Professional football quarterback] Michael Vick could have used his fame to influence countless boys and girls in a positive manner, instead of spending his spare time running a dogfighting ring, getting caught with illegal drugs and allegedly giving women herpes. His dogfighting ring was called Bad Newz Kennels, which is appropriate, since Vick himself was bad news. Now instead of living in a mansion and playing on national television on Sundays, Vick resides in the federal penitentiary in Leavenworth, Kan.

Athletes Can Make a Difference

Meanwhile, another former quarterback who wore No. 7, Danny Wuerffel, is a role model. Wuerffel won the Heisman Trophy in 1996, when he led Florida to the national championship, and went on to play six seasons in the NFL. He used his fame and the money he earned in the NFL to help underprivileged children in inner-city New Orleans. Desire Street Ministries is a non-profit faith-based organization located in one of the poorest areas of New Orleans. It focuses on spiritual and community development. It is an organization that is making a difference in the lives of kids who desperately need it.

The sports world needs more Warrick Dunns and fewer Pacman Joneses [professional football players]. Both grew up poor in low-income neighborhoods. Dunn chose to stay out of trouble and try to better himself, through sports and academics, while Jones did not.

Dunn, one of only a handful of running backs in NFL history to rush for over 10,000 yards, owns a degree from Florida State, a football career he can definitely be proud of, and a history of charity work that has made a big difference in the lives of those he has helped. Dunn's charity, the Warrick Dunn Foundation, is focused primarily on helping devoted single parents purchase a home for the first time (something his late mother, a policewoman killed in the line of duty, was never able to do). As of last December [2007], the program has helped 74 single parents and 192 dependents achieve the goal of owning their own home for the first time.

Jones should not be proud of the life he's led. The suspended Tennessee Titans cornerback frequents strip clubs— never a place for a true role model to go—and has had several brushes with the law. He has been known to hang around with an entourage of thugs, one of which shot an innocent bystander while in Jones' company last year. His behavior, both on the field and off the field, has been bad enough that NFL commissioner Roger Goodell suspended him for the entire 2007 season.

I am definitely a fan of men like Wuerffel and Dunn, who understand that they can use their celebrity to have a positive influence.

I am a fan of men like Dunn, Wuerffel, Charlie Ward, David Robinson and Tim Duncan, men who have had long, scandal-free pro sports careers, while also doing extensive charity work. These five are also men who got their college degrees, another reason I would call them role models.

I am also a big fan of Valdosta's [Georgia] own Randall Godfrey, a man who has been a good role model for our local kids. Godfrey, a star at Lowndes High and Georgia, has played 12 years in the NFL, and has also been scandal free. Godfrey holds a camp for local kids every June at Lowndes, and is another athlete that does a lot of charity work.

Gifted Athletes Should Give Back

On the other hand, I am saddened by men like Vick and Jones, who could be making a difference, but instead hang around with the wrong crowd, do things they shouldn't do, and make foolish decisions that get them in trouble. People like them help give athletes a bad rap.

There are many other examples in the sports world of good role models and bad role models. I hope most of us will choose to root for the good guys.

Being a star athlete is a great privilege that many of us dream of, and few actually achieve. It takes a lot of God-given talent and a lot of work to reach that goal.

Those lucky enough to achieve that goal need to use that status in positive ways.

> "But it is on that singular and limited
> dimension, as an example or model of
> the specific role of the athlete, that we
> should judge our professional athletes,
> and no more."

Athletes Should Be Role Models Only for Athletics

Jeffrey Standen

Jeffrey Standen, professor of law at Willamette University in Oregon, maintains in the following viewpoint that professional athletes are indeed role models, but not in an unlimited sense; they are role models for the specific role of athlete. According to Standen, children should idolize athletes for such characteristics as their commitment to the sport, their physical ability, and their pursuit of excellence, but the public should not demand that athletes be role models for non-athletic virtues such as humility or generosity.

As you read, consider the following questions:

1. What is the important limitation about the definition of "role model," according to the author?

Jeffrey Standen, "Athletes as Role Models," The Sports Law Professor Blog, July 29, 2007. Reproduced by permission.

2. Does Jeffrey Standen believe that because fans buy tickets to watch athletes play, athletes owe it to the public to exhibit high moral standards?

3. Does the behavior of high-profile athletes contribute to the demise of professional sports or to their success, according to Standen?

With an NBA [National Basketball Association] referee facing game-fixing accusations, pro quarterback Michael Vick accused of dog-fighting and suspended from the NFL, and Barry Bonds' home-run record having brought to the fore baseball's perduing problem with steroids, now seems as bad a time as any to reconsider the bromide about superstar athletes serving as role models for youngsters. Should parents point to these law-breaking, drug-ingesting, bet-placing, fan-despising, spoiled, pampered rich athletes and tell our children to be like them? Are athletes role models? Are they good ones?

Yes, on all counts.

Understanding the Definition of "Role Model"

First let's define "role model." It's not just "model," it's a model of a specific "role." This is an important limitation. None of us are models for children in an unlimited sense; even we parents should be humble enough to hope that our children do not mirror our behaviors completely. We all want our kids to share in our good qualities, not the bad.

Athletes are role models for children, but only for the role of "athlete." Athletes display the athletic virtues: diligence, perseverance, the value of training, fair play and sportsmanship, grace under pressure, and the pursuit of excellence. The best of our athletes exhibit these virtues abundantly, in full public display. How familiar is the story of the gifted athlete whose rise to stardom is fueled by endless practice, peak performance on notable college teams, and diligent perfecting of his professional game? How common is the athlete who has over-come a deeply difficult upbringing in single- or no-parent homes amidst neighborhood poverty and crime? This time of year I daily help my young children organize themselves to ar-rive on time, fed and properly dressed for baseball practice. What chance would my kids have were a parent not available to make sports participation easy? It amazes me that many of our accomplished professional athletes were able to put it all together and excel. One can watch any professional game in any sport and see role models at every position.

Wanting More than a "Role" Model

Yet some fans and commentators apparently want more. They want athletes to be more than a model of a role; they want athletes to be a model of all personal and public virtues. Why should we expect athletes to exhibit non-athletic virtues to any greater degree than we or others model such qualities? Virtues such as honesty, integrity, self-control, humility, kind-ness, generosity and the like are immensely important, but they are no more important to the athlete than they are to the rest of us. Why should I expect to point to an athlete or other celebrity to show my children an example of humility or gen-erosity, more than I should live a life where I can point to my-self? But when the lesson is about the pursuit of excellence and the need to practice or the possibility of overcoming ob-stacles or the determination needed to succeed, well, profes-sional sports players are exemplars. What more can we ask of them? That a person pursuing his own life's goals can unin-tentionally be a paragon of excellence for others is the best role model possible.

Of course some athletes fail to model the role that they have assumed and that we can rightfully expect from them. We can't fairly ask our sports stars to be especially kind or honest, but we can ask them to exhibit good sportsmanship and a commitment to fair play. I am personally dubious about

Too Bright a Spotlight for Some Athletes

There was a time athletes could be role models because the media protected them.... Today, it's different. Parents cannot expect athletes to give direction to their kids. First, athletes are [constantly] under the glare of the camera. Secondly, [some] athletes use their celebrity to promote outrageous behavior—like Dennis Rodman, Terrell Owens, and Latrell Sprewell. We have a whole different class of athlete. In a sense, many of them are the antithesis of what is required of a role model.

Congressman Emanuel Cleaver II
in an interview with George J. Tanber,
"Cleaver: Not All Athletes Are Role Models,"
ESPN.com, February 7, 2007.

the logic behind the ban on performance enhancements, for example, but rules are rules, and players who flout the rules cheat the game, much as talented players who squander their innate gifts cheat the duty they owe to their employers and, by extension, their fans. Athletes are models for their roles, and like any role model they can succeed or fail at that role. But it is on that singular and limited dimension, as an example or model of the specific role of the athlete, that we should judge our professional athletes, and no more.

Admiring the Athlete as an Athlete

Children understand my point implicitly. I can point to [professional basketball player] Kobe Bryant's wonderful form on a jump shot as worthy of emulation without my children taking my comment as an implicit endorsement of Bryant's broken adherence to his marital vow. I can (one day perhaps) mention Michael Vick's success as an NFL [National Football League] quarterback to evidence the possibility for a person to overcome certain physical limitations (in his case, inferior height for the position) and perform athletic tasks competently, and do so without endorsing mistreatment of helpless animals. And so on. I suspect strongly that the claimed worry about kids ("What can we tell our children?") that one hears when the foibles and errors of star athletes are once again brought to public light is nothing more than an invention, something we say because we can't bring ourselves to speak the truth.

Taking Responsibility for Ourselves

The truth is this: we're not really worried about our children. We fans should worry about ourselves. We have it in mind that we have a right to spy, pry and obsess about the private lives of people who "choose" certain occupations, such as athlete or movie star, and deep down we know this is voyeurism. And then we think that our decision to watch them (and spy and pry) justifies our holding them to a standard that we ourselves do not always meet. And that if they, the stars, don't like our spying and prying, then they (we say) should not have chosen to be in the public arena. Wrong. We watchers made the choice to watch, and it's a new decision each time we buy a ticket to the game or turn on the television. The basketball player will play (if that's his best occupation) whether it's in front of a small crowd or an international television audience. The player chooses to expose that much of his life (his playing of the game) to our scrutiny. The rest of the prying and spying is clearly not the athlete's choice; it's ours. Should we be surprised when that part of the athlete's life that the athlete did not choose to be held open to public scrutiny fails to measure up to the virtuous excellence we want to see (and very often do see) on the playing field or court?

We should be ashamed of ourselves for our constant, envious nosiness into what is often not our business. All of us "go public" with certain aspects of our lives, if only to advertise our businesses, apply for a job, or write a book. Should that limited act of consent mean that all aspects of our life are now fair game for the prying eye? If not, then why should this be the case for the athlete?

Of course it's news and newsworthy when a high-profile athlete is accused of a serious crime or of cheating the game, much as would be the case for any other citizen. But our legitimate interest in the private lives of our celebrity athletes does not go much further. We need to allow these young men and women to try and fail at the "non-athletic" human virtues as much as we permit everybody else. We ask enough of these athletes to achieve perfection in the athletic virtues. That they accomplish these athletic virtues so often and under such pressure is testament not to the demise of professional sports in this country, but to their success. Long gone are the days of baseball players drinking beer during games or basketball players using cocaine before the tipoff. Few today are the gifted athletes who negligently or lazily squander away their talent. Our professional athletes are more virtuous and yes, better role models than they have ever been. That we fans and observers fail to recognize this, and instead demand even more of them, creates a vision of a "role model" that is unrealistic and unreasonable.

> "Sport is holistic in its benefits, promoting physical growth as much as helping children develop social skills and self-confidence."

Sports Can Benefit Children with Disabilities

Brady Delander

In the following viewpoint, Brady Delander explains that just about every sport can be adapted for children with disabilities so that all kids can reap the benefits of participating in sports. According to Delander, many children with disabilities believe they are unable to play sports or do not even try for fear of injury or of being ridiculed by other kids. He further maintains that once children with disabilities move beyond their fear and give sports a try, their physical agility and strength will improve and their self-esteem will skyrocket. Brady Delander is a writer living in Denver, Colorado.

As you read, consider the following questions:

1. According to Brady Delander, why do parents sometimes hold back their children from playing sports?

Brady Delander, "Better than Spinach: Young Minds and Muscles Benefit Equally with Activity," *The O&P Edge*, April 2008. Reproduced with permission of Western Media, LLC.

2. Robin Burton, coordinator of "First" programs, says that socialization for kids with disabilities is as important as physical activity. What does she mean by that?

3. Should someone with just one leg be discouraged from learning to ski, according to Delander?

Michael McHugh was afraid to fall and hurt himself. Growing up, those concerns held him back from almost any kind of activity or athletic event that he perceived as daunting. Fear of injury, falling, failing, or whatever can be a major deterrent for those with physical disabilities, or anyone else for that matter, but the beauty of sport and athletic activity is that it overcomes fear first. Once that is accomplished, the benefits of exercise extend beyond the body to the mind and soul.

McHugh, now a high school senior in Cortland Manor, New York, vanquished his fears by facing them head on, turning what seemed impossible into the ordinary. "I used to stay away from sports, take a backseat," says McHugh, a 17-year-old born with arthrogryposis, which essentially shriveled the tendons and inhibited muscle growth in his legs. "When I was younger I was terrified of falling, terrified of heights. I think falling is the scariest thing for any disabled person." Born with dislocated hips and feet turned backward and upside-down, doctors decided to cut the tendons and swivel his feet forward, fusing McHugh's ankles at a 90-degree angle to his legs. He uses an ankle-foot orthosis (AFO) on each leg and crutches to get around. Before hitting the slopes at age nine, McHugh tended to be a wallflower.

"Skiing in particular has given me a lot more confidence," says McHugh, who tries to ski at least once a week while the snow is good. "Physically I'm stronger, and I have better balance. Mentally I know that I can do anything that I set my mind to."

The message for parents of children with physical disabilities is to get them involved with some type of athletic activity and the younger the better.

Sports Are Good for the Mind and Body

The physical gain is obvious and beneficial. "If you take a sedentary child and turn [him] into an active child that is, of course, good," says Pam Greene, program director for the Adaptive Sports Foundation (ASF), Windham Mountain, New York. "Sports and exercise can improve things like balance, flexibility, agility, and strength, and that carries over to a better quality of life day to day."

A little sweat benefits the mind as well. Ringing the bell at the top of a rock-climbing wall or hitting a tennis ball over the net a few times builds self-esteem and confidence, and those feats help children with disabilities to see themselves in a new light. "The increase in self esteem is huge, as is the awareness of their own abilities," says Cindy Housner, executive director of the Great Lakes Adaptive Sports Association, Lake Forest, Illinois. "Sometimes a young person might not have a certain amount of self confidence or social skills, but sports give them the opportunity to get in the game. It allows them to pursue life skills and become successful in the community."

Oftentimes it is the parents who are reluctant to get their kids involved in sports, and their reason is usually the same one that gripped a young McHugh before he learned to conquer snow-covered mountains: fear. "Parents can be hesitant. They might be concerned that their child will get hurt, or they just don't understand how much good can come from getting involved," Housner says.

However, since kids are kids, even informed and motivated parents might have difficulty convincing their child to climb into a mono-ski or jump into the swimming pool for the first time. "So many of the kids, especially the younger ones, they

Pushing for a Title X

Disabled kids are often shut out of that quintessential high school experience unless they're content to watch from the bleachers.

But a Berkeley activist is trying to change that. Rick Spittler, who's worked for 30 years to bring sports and outdoor recreation to disabled people, has set his sights on the schoolyard. . . .

"No significant change is going to take place until a specific law addresses this issue," he said. "I think the time is right for this. . . . I think we can make it happen."

Carolyn Jones, "Pushing for Disabled Kids
to Have an Equal Shot at School Sports,"
San Francisco Chronicle, *November 5, 2007.*

say no to everything. When you first ask them if they want to ski or swim or play basketball, they say no. I tell the parents, 'Please don't listen to your kid,'" Housner says, laughing. "There are so many activities; there is a fit for everyone."

There Is a Sport for Everyone

Every state in the United States has at least one adaptive sport program, and the numbers are growing. . . .

In addition, the Orthotic and Prosthetic Assistance Fund Inc. (OPAF), has garnered recognition for its "First" programs, which are held across the country and provide children and others with disabilities a chance to try a number of adaptive activities, including golf, tennis, and swimming. "Socialization for these kids is equal to the physical activity," says Robin Burton, executive director for OPAF and coordinator of First events across the country. "An event like this is often the first time a child will see someone who is like them. We've been just about everywhere, and it seems like there is always someplace else to go."

And it seems that there is no sport that cannot be adapted for a child with disabilities. Snow skiing is prevalent in mountain states, and the benefits involved with carving through powder at a high rate of speed with the wind blowing in your face are bountiful. "I was an instructor for a young cancer patient who lost a leg, and the first comment he made after skiing was, 'That's the fastest I've ever been able to go on my own,'" says Tom Trevithick, educational director and equipment manager for ASF, and a Professional Ski Instructors of America (PSIA) level III adaptive and alpine ski instructor. A knee-disarticulation amputee, Trevithick understands the need for speed. "As an amputee, you feel like you can't do as many things as the able-bodied, and you can't really. But you put a ski on and you can move on your own, as fast as you want."

Whether in the mountains, by the sea, or anywhere in between, almost any sport or activity can provide equally spectacular results. "There are a lot of activities out there that are easily adaptive, depending on the individual—running, cardio, swimming, basketball, even rock climbing." Housner says.

Just as a child might turn up her nose at the sight and smell of spinach on her dinner plate, so might she turn away from, say, a game of basketball or a dip in the pool. Taking a turn on the dance floor, however, might pique her interest. Those interviewed for this article agree that any activity that holds a child's attention is the right one. "What makes an adaptive sport successful is finding something that the kids themselves are interested in," says Derrick Stowell, MS [master of science], CTRS [certified therapeutic recreation specialist], coordinator of the Amputee Coalition of America's (ACA) Youth Activities Program (YAP).

Stowell recounted a story from the YAP camp last summer of one youngster with upper-extremity limb differences who had decided that his disability would prevent him from taking part. Stowell wanted the boy to give tennis or disc golf a try, but the camper didn't think it was possible. "He said, 'I can't do this. I don't have any arms, so there's nothing I can do,'" Stowell says. "I talked with him a little bit and explained that part of the reason he was here was to try something you don't think you can do."

After a bit of trial and error adaptation, as Stowell says the youngster found a way to toss the disc, and at the same time he squashed his doubts about being able to participate.

The Benefits of Sports Are Profound

Sport is holistic in its benefits, promoting physical growth as much as helping children develop social skills and self-confidence. An obvious question, maybe, but what is it about sports that opens so many doors?

"Ask yourself," says Shauna Smith-Vladimiross, CTRS, a recreational therapist for Sun Valley Adaptive Sports in Ketchum, Idaho. "When you first picked up a sport and mastered it, how did you feel? It felt like it changed everything... You accomplished a personal goal. It was fun and time flew. You forgot all your worries. For anybody, disabled or not, recreation is a great tool that carries over into everyday life."

Smith-Vladimiross talked about a young girl with severe autism as well as Larsen Syndrome, a condition characterized by congenital dislocation of multiple joints in the body, among other issues who would only communicate with screams, cries, and grumbles. The Sun Valley crew convinced the girl to try a run in a sit-ski. When she returned the next year, she was skiing on her own. "She was completely independent, wearing skis and boots and going downhill standing up," Smith-Vladimiross says. "And she was communicating more. She'd say, 'Go,' or 'boots on.' That was huge."

Athletes with Disabilities Deserve the Same Support as Able-bodied Athletes

Mastering an individual sport is indeed an accomplishment to be proud of, but some kids might crave an added element of fierce competition. The Atlanta-based American Association of Adapted Sports Programs (AAASP), co-founded by Bev Vaughn and Tommie Storms, is the only state-sanctioned athletic association in the country that serves students with physical disabilities, though Alabama and New Jersey have begun to examine the institution of similar systems. Vaughn and Storms have done for young athletes with disabilities in Georgia what Patsy Mink [U.S. Representative from Hawaii who authored the Title IX Amendment of the Higher Education Act] did for female student-athletes with the Title IX equality act in 1972. That means high school students in Georgia on the wheelchair basketball team receive the same perks as the players on the able-bodied varsity squad, including a televised state championship game.

"The kids on these teams are just like their non-disabled peers; the uniforms, equipment, state tournaments," says Vaughn, AAASP's executive director. "The fitness level and the confidence level translate back to the classroom. Grades and academic performance improves, secondary health problems decrease, and behavioral problems decrease."

AAASP is now well-established in Georgia, benefitting 4,000 disabled student-athletes over the past ten years, but it wasn't easy in the beginning. Funding was and remains the top priority, but Vaughn rattled off a long list of other issues that had to be tackled in order to let the games begin: standardized equipment; adapted rules for each sport; and a training curriculum for coaches. She now has her sights set on the national scene.

"The challenges are daunting, but we want to ensure that these types of activities are available everywhere there is a need," Vaughn says.

Efforts like AAASP, as well as events such as the O&P [Orthotics and Prosthetics] Extremity Games have lifted the curtain on what is possible for young persons with disabilities. That fact isn't lost on McHugh, whose eyes were opened once he challenged himself on the ski slopes.

"I know that I can do any sport as a physically disabled person and that any sport can be adapted for the physically disabled," McHugh says.

Periodical Bibliography

The following articles have been selected to supplement the diverse views presented in this chapter.

Erin Allday	"The Growing Pains of Childhood Sports Injuries," *San Francisco Chronicle*, March 7, 2008.
Associated Press	"Should Athletes with Disabilities Be Allowed to Compete in AB Sporting Events?" January 14, 2008.
Grace Baranowski	"Athletes Aren't Paid to Be Role Models," *Hi-Lite*, September 7, 2007.
Marcia Bradford	"Changing Lives: How Sports Planners Are Impacting Youth for Life," *Sports Events*, May 2008.
Bill Dickens	"Once Troubled Teen Finds His Way Through Football," *San Diego Union-Tribune*, June 5, 2008.
Judy Foreman	"Women Athletes Win Equal Time on Injury List," *Boston Globe*, April 14, 2008.
Joe Mannion	"Raising Healthy Child Athletes: The 'Good-Enough' Coach & Parent," *AllWorld Performance*, March 2007.
Christine Mueller	"Racing to a Degree: High School Sports Help Girls Earn College Diplomas," *U.S. News & World Report*, August 6, 2007.
Jeffrey Thomas	"Equality in Sports Participation Benefits All, Says Expert: Girls Benefit in Academic and Professional Life," America.gov, April 17, 2008.
Tucker Center for Research on Girls & Women in Sport	"The 2007 Tucker Center Research Report: Developing Physically Active Girls," 2007.
Russell Williams	"Athletes as Role Models for Character," *Albuquerque Tribune*, June 27, 2007.

CHAPTER 2

Should College Sports Be Reformed?

Chapter Preface

In 2005, National Basketball Association (NBA) Commissioner David Stern imposed a new eligibility rule regarding high school players. The rule, which took effect with the 2006 NBA draft, stipulates that (1) all players must be at least nineteen years of age during the calendar year of the draft; and (2) a player must be at least one year removed from the graduation of his high school class. In essence, a high school basketball player with aspirations and talent for playing in the NBA must attend at least one year of college. Stern believes this rule has the best interests of young athletes in mind because it gives them one more year to develop physically as well as mentally before playing among some of America's best athletes, who are older and presumably stronger. However, the rule has produced much controversy and dissension among potential NBA draftees, parents, players, coaches, recruiters—practically everyone associated with professional basketball.

Bill Walker, a basketball player who wanted to bypass college and go directly to the NBA from high school, said, "I'm against it. I don't see why you have to be nineteen to play a game of basketball when you can be eighteen and go to war for our country and die. It's ridiculous." Jerryd Bayless, a basketball player who left college basketball after one year to sign with the Portland Trail Blazers, agrees with Walker. "It's not fair at all. If a tennis player can go pro at thirteen, I don't understand why a basketball player can't go pro at eighteen." And Billy Donovan, basketball coach at the University of Florida, said, "The way the whole thing is set up now, it's not good for anybody. I think it would make our game a lot better if kids didn't have to go to college. . . . This one-year thing we have, it's like a pit stop for nine months."

Turning college into a "pit stop" is one of the major points of opposition to the rule. Critics contend it makes a mockery of higher education, and that it uses college scholarships to provide training camps for the NBA, similar to the way major league baseball uses its minor leagues. Basketball analyst Brad G. Faye expressed his view in a July 2008 newsroom debate posted on the Phoenix Suns Web site: "College is not an obligation; it is a privilege. And I think imposing this rule wastes scholarships on players who go the route of 'one-and-done' as opposed to a guy who, while not as talented, actually wants to benefit from receiving an education while also playing basketball."

Supporters of the rule, however, insist that it favorably serves both the potential draftees as well as the NBA, so much so that many would like to see the minimum age requirement raised even higher. These advocates believe high school players would benefit from playing college basketball for a year or two to enhance their skills and better prepare them to play professionally. They cite many players, such as Leon Smith and Korleone Young, who were drafted right out of high school and subsequently failed to succeed in the NBA. Professional basketball player Brandon Wright said of the rule, "It may hurt guys who need money, but it will help people grow and develop." And in response to the critics who point to tennis players, gymnasts, and ice skaters who become professionals in their early teens, basketball analyst Dan Hilton said, "I think the main difference is those athletes are depending on their own talent and aren't banging bodies against adults who are much older and developed than they are. Playing a sport where you are just looking at your opponent is much different than one where you have to physically match up against your opponent and try to score or defend. Giving the high school kids just one more year to continue to grow and mature makes a lot of difference."

It remains to be seen how the controversy over the NBA eligibility rule will play out, whether it will remain intact or be reformed. In the following chapter, the authors examine other issues concerning college sports and what, if anything, should be reformed.

> *"Today, the roles and enforced environment that both the schools themselves and the National Collegiate Athletic Association (NCAA) use to guide college athletics are far too strict for students to merely skate by."*

Academic Achievement Is Improving for College Athletes

Doug Jolley

In the following viewpoint, Doug Jolley contends that the Academic Performance Rate (APR)—part of a program implemented by the National Collegiate Athletic Association (NCAA) to ensure that scholarship student athletes meet specific academic levels—has resulted in education becoming a priority for student athletes. Jolley notes that athletic and academic professionals at the University of South Carolina, University of Georgia, and Clemson in South Carolina are encouraged by the emphasis on academics and believe that the majority of their student athletes will graduate. Doug Jolley, a former professional football player, is a columnist for the sports publishing company Scout.com.

As you read, consider the following questions:

1. What does the Academic Performance Rate measure, according to the author?

2. According to Doug Jolley, what methods do the University of South Carolina, University of Georgia, and Clemson University use to support their at-risk athletes?

3. The National Collegiate Athletic Association structured the APR so that Division I (schools with the largest enrollment) student athletes progress toward what goal, according to Jolley?

One of the biggest changes in the history of college athletics was the adoption of the Academic Performance Rate [APR] by the NCAA [National Collegiate Athletic Association]. It established goals for graduating student-athletes, and schools and their athletic programs are subject to severe penalties if they don't meet them. How has the APR changed college athletics? Just ask the people responsible for meeting those goals. . . .

Say you're a highly coveted athlete, and you've just chosen one school over all the others clamoring for your services. Now all you have to look forward to is competing as an athlete, and finding all those incredible parties everyone hears about, right? The reality of what being a student-athlete really means can be culture shock when a student walks onto campus and into a structured environment that, in many cases, fairly compares to the military academies.

Improved Academic Support for Student Athletes

The time demands on a student-athlete are daunting, with weight training frequently starting as early as 6 a.m.; then add to that class schedules, 20 hours/week of practice time during the season, study time each week, traveling to athletic events, and finally actually playing the sport in which they compete.

If you want your child to excel at the college level and graduate from college, one of your best bets is to encourage them to compete as an athlete in any sport at a major college. As previously stated, college student-athletes lead incredibly busy lives, and the structure and support provided for them to help them succeed academically in the midst of all their responsibilities is unparalleled elsewhere in academia.

It hasn't always been that way. The stories in the past of nearly illiterate athletes graduating from college after spending their school days focused primarily on athletics were often true. Today [2008], the rules and enforced environment that both the schools themselves and the National Collegiate Athletic Association (NCAA) use to guide college athletics are far too strict for students to merely skate by.

This ... [article focuses] on three different universities—South Carolina [USC], Georgia [UGA], and Clemson—and how they currently are working diligently to help their student-athletes meet their academic goals and requirements, as well as stay eligible to compete athletically. The NCAA these days is making sure of it, with the Academic Performance Rate (APR) putting the bite in their bark. The APR measures academic performance and retention each fall and spring throughout their college careers.

Effect of the APR

One Bulldog [mascot for UGA] who is in charge of keeping his students and his school away from that bite is UGA's Ted White. He is the director of Georgia's Academic Center for Student-Athletes, the Rankin Smith Sr. Center. He held a similar position at LSU [Louisiana State University] before coming to UGA.

White said, "It has been incredible. The attention and emphasis now on academics I think is due to the APR. You are being measured now. You are being measured publicly, nationally. In the conference, everyone is going to want to know

APR Trends in Baseball, Men's Basketball and Football

The Academic Progress Rate is trending upward overall, and real improvement is most obvious in the sports of baseball and football. While men's basketball still has some progress to make, the most recent year's data shows a small gain.

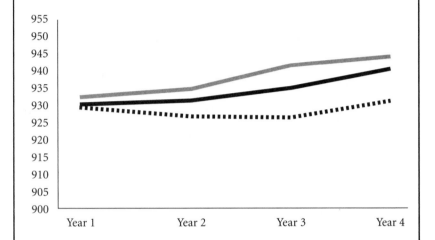

■■ Baseball
■ Football
■■■ Men's Basketball

Note: Analyses based on 281 baseball squads, 325 men's basketball squads and 233 football squads that sponsored the sport within Division 1 during all four years.

TAKEN FROM: National Collegiate Athletic Association, "Reform's Inroads Evident with APR Release," May 6, 2008.

what that score is. What is the health of your academic program? It has been terrific in terms of getting people's attention on the campuses—at LSU and here—the attention of the administration on campus and the Athletic Department. We are fortunate here in that they pay close attention to it and that they are very determined that the student-athletes have a great academic experience, and that those numbers bear that out."

The head Bulldog regarding compliance with the APR is Glada Horvat, the Assistant Athletic Director for Academics and Eligibility at Georgia. "Coaches pay attention to it, I can tell you that," Horvat said. "We hope that they take that into account when they make recruiting decisions on students, because ultimately they're going to have to pay a price for students coming in and not being successful. I believe the APR makes them very careful about the students they choose to recruit. They still take academic risk, but they have to be careful that they are not taking a large number of them and people that they can be sure can 'take care of business,' and they're going to have to stay on top of those people too."

South Carolina Athletic Director Eric Hyman was emphatic about the impact of the APR on college athletics. "I've said all along that this issue has and will continue to have the biggest impact of my professional career. I don't know that people really grasp or understand it yet. Some people are, but I've been harping on it for nine years now. Why have I been involved in building two academic enrichment centers prior to coming here? There's a reason. How it's going to look like five years from now, I can't answer that question. There's no question that the APR is going to change the culture." Hyman is overseeing the development of a new academic enrichment center for student-athletes at USC as well.

More Student Athletes Graduate

Val Sheley, USC's Senior Associate Athletic Director, talked about the correlation between increasingly higher admissions standards and the APR, and how they affect both recruiting and the subsequent graduation of student-athletes. "The fact that we have higher admissions than the NCAA requires makes it more difficult in some aspects of recruiting. But ultimately, the process we have now will ensure that the vast majority of our kids that come here are going to be successful. You're always going to get one or two that will be a surprise. But I really believe that if they can meet the standards, with the help of the coaching and Academic Center staffs, and with the right attitude even the academically challenged can graduate."

South Carolina, Georgia, and Clemson all have a system of tutors and mentors for the student-athlete. Georgia has learning specialists like April Thompson to help their at-risk athletes. "I work with the student-athlete's learning disabilities and deficiencies, and teach them how to be successful in college." Thompson said. "Things that come easy for us, they have never done before—study skills like highlighting, or making note cards. We teach them those skills. We take their learning style, whether it is auditory, visual, or kinesthetic, and teach them the tricks of the trade that work based on their individual learning style."

Former NCAA official and current Clemson Athletic Director for Academic Services Becky Bowman took a slightly different tack on the APR. "I don't think that it's really changed how we do business at Vickery Hall," she said. "We've always set out to have a very comprehensive academic support service. We've always set out to help our scholarship and our walk-on student-athletes earn a degree, and we just continue to provide that support to them. We have a special program for some of our student-athletes who have come in at-risk because they haven't picked up all the tools that would help them be competitive in our academic environment here. We have a mentor program. We have an advisor that's assigned to every one of our teams. It really has not changed what we do."

How the APR Works

The NCAA structured the APR as a way to be sure that Division 1 student-athletes are genuinely making progress toward graduation. It gives them added information on student-athletes and their academic performance so that they are able to better enforce the rules.

APR hurts a team when student-athletes don't remain in school, or remain but are ineligible. Each athletic scholarship student-athlete can earn a total of 4 points per year, 1 point for eligibility and 1 point for retention each fall and spring term. All the points are calibrated over a four year period and the magic number is 925. If a team's APR is 925 or over, they are fine. However, if the score is less than 925, a team can be subject to contemporaneous penalties. That means if you have any student-athletes left ineligible, that scholarship cannot be re-awarded to someone else for a year.

There are some exceptions. For instance, if a student-athlete leaves for a professional career, but is eligible when he leaves, he does not hurt his team. For example, [basketball player] Renaldo Balkman and [football player] Sidney Rice leaving their teams for a professional career did not hurt South Carolina because they were both eligible to return to USC. The other magic number is 900. If a team scores below 900, they are subject to historical penalties that get more severe each year the team score is below 900. This can result in loss of scholarships, practice/competition time, and eventually NCAA membership if a pattern of improvement cannot be provided over a four year period.

USC head football coach Steve Spurrier addressed a specific situation this spring when discussing two fifth-year seniors, twins Dustin and Jordin Lindsey: "If the Lindsey boys pass and do what they're supposed to do, they've got a chance to graduate and play next year," Spurrier said. "They've got a little work to do to be eligible. But they certainly can do it. We're hoping they will. If they don't make it, it hurts your APR points."

Sheley wrapped up discussion of the APR by saying, "This isn't a flash in the pan that's going to come and go, and there isn't a way to get you out of this. When dealing with NCAA legislation, there are a lot of instances when a waiver can be sought. To some extent you can do that with APR, but the circumstances have to be extreme and you have to be able to show a plan for improvement. These types of waivers are going to be far more difficult to attain. If, at the end of the day, when all the points are added up and all the calculations are done, and a team is under 900 or a team is under 925, there is no waiver out of that."

"'When there's pressure applied you're going to get a reaction, and the reaction we're seeing is academic fraud cases.'"

Academic Fraud Is Rampant in College Athletics

Elia Powers

Elia Powers explains in the following viewpoint how the academic reform measures implemented by the National Collegiate Athletic Association (NCAA) have led to an increased likelihood of academic fraud. Powers asserts that many experts are concerned that holding student athletes accountable for higher academic standards in order to maintain eligibility puts considerable pressure on coaches, athletic departments, support groups, and the athletes themselves—often to the point of encouraging educators to change test scores or offer watered-down courses. Elia Powers is a reporter and staff writer for Inside Higher Ed, *a Web site that covers national higher education issues.*

As you read, consider the following questions:

1. According to the author, why did the NCAA set new academic rules regarding student athletes?

Elia Powers, "Academic Fraud in Collegiate Athletics," InsideHigherEd.com, October 2, 2007. Reproduced by permission.

2. Upon setting the academic progress rules, did the NCAA raise or lower college entrance requirements, according to Elia Powers?

3. Does the NCAA believe that the focus should be primarily on what students achieved academically in high school or on what they will be able to achieve in college?

Academic fraud cases have long been a staple of the National Collegiate Athletic Association's infractions list. The descriptions are pleasure reading for critics of big-time college sports who bemoan the influence that determined athletics officials, administrators and faculty can have on keeping athletes eligible at all costs.

Of late, there's been no shortage of material:

- At Florida State University, a "learning specialist" and a tutor "perpetrated academic dishonesty" in a scandal involving 23 athletes, an internal investigation found. In some cases, the employees—both of whom resigned, according to the university—gave students answers to online exams and typed material for them.

- A former Purdue University women's basketball assistant coach, fired last year [2006], was found to have partially researched and composed a sociology paper for a player and then lied about it to university officials who were looking into the allegations. The coach left an e-mail trail behind that proved to be the smoking gun.

- The University of Kansas received three years' probation last fall [2006] for a series of violations, including a former graduate assistant football coach who gave two prospective athletes answers to test questions for correspondence courses they were taking at the university.

- Add to the list concerns over correspondence courses that allow athletes to gain eligibility and the issue of "clustering"—illustrated in the Auburn University case involving a sociology professor who is accused of offering specialized classes to athletes that required little work.

Whether or not cases of academic fraud have become more rampant or even more serious in recent years is open to debate; statistics on their occurrence (increased or otherwise) are hard to come by. But many agree that the climate has changed in college athletics in ways that may make such misbehavior more likely. And it has happened since the NCAA unveiled its latest set of academic policies that raised the stakes on colleges to show that their athletes perform well in the classroom while simultaneously lowering the requirements freshman athletes must meet to become eligible initially.

Pressure to Meet Academic Levels Is Great

Largely as a response to sagging graduation rates for football and basketball players, the NCAA put into place several years ago new academic rules that require colleges to report each term whether their athletes are on progress toward a degree— with penalties awaiting those whose students aren't progressing and aren't performing.

At the same time, the NCAA reversed its previous approach of continually raising initial entrance requirements and began allowing students with SAT [scholastic aptitude test] scores as low as 400 (or a corresponding ACT [college aptitude test] score) to enroll so long as their high school grades were high enough. That move appeased critics of the standardized test score requirement who said it adversely affected minority students.

In the years since the changes, many have expressed concern that the combination of heightened academic expectations and lowered entrance regulations would put the campus

"I could have gone to college on an athletic scholarship, but they found out I could read."

©Marty Bucella/Cartoonstock.com.

employees responsible for providing academic support to athletes in a tough spot, asked to help a growing number of marginal students—potentially at all costs.

That fear is so real to James F. Barker, president of Clemson University, that he meets each semester with everyone who gives tutorial help or guidance to athletes and "reads them the Riot Act."

"I tell them, 'I'm responsible for 20,000 people and a half-a-billion-dollar budget—those two things could keep me awake at night, but they don't. What does is academic fraud. No student-athlete is worth crossing that line for,'" says Barker, who also heads the NCAA's Division I Board of Directors, the panel of college presidents that governs the NCAA's highest-profile competitive level.

Experts Disagree on the Academic Reform Measures

David Goldfield, a professor of history at the University of North Carolina at Charlotte who served on the academic eligibility and compliance cabinet of the NCAA, which helped craft the new policy, said he supports the new progress standards but still opposes lowering entrance requirements—which he said strains the entire system of academic support.

"When there's pressure applied you're going to get a reaction, and the reaction we're seeing is academic fraud cases," Goldfield said. "From a coach's perspective, the major task is to win, but now with the new requirements, the second and often equally pressing task is to maintain the eligibility of players."

Goldfield fears that academic fraud cases are far more widespread than just the ones reported to the NCAA. Compliance officers can have a difficult time tracking down such cases, he said, because they can involve wrongdoing by people in all parts of an institution, and often rely on self-reporting by athletics officials.

The NCAA did not have a comment for this article. Kevin Lennon, the association's vice president for membership services, said in a statement about the Florida State case that "the NCAA and its member institutions take seriously any allegation of academic misconduct" and that "these types of violations are among the most serious that can be committed."

Lennon added that the NCAA is committed to its academic reform measures. The association has defended its eligibility changes by arguing that the focus should be primarily on what students can achieve in college and not just on their high school academic performance.

Some Student Athletes Are Unprepared Academically for College

But some say that stance ignores the reality that unprepared students often can't cut it in college.

"Just because you're technically eligible to compete doesn't mean you are ready to compete in the classroom," said Tim Metcalf, director of compliance at East Carolina University.

Terry Holland, a longtime men's basketball coach at the University of Virginia who is now athletics director at East Carolina, said coaches and college officials are under increasing pressure to accept any student who qualifies under the NCAA's rules. In his meetings with other athletics directors, Holland said he hasn't encountered one yet who says athletes are better prepared now than they were five years ago.

"For many programs, the recruiting pitch is, 'We have a great academic support system and everyone graduates,'" Holland said. "Maybe what the athletes are hearing is, 'You're going to do the work for me. It may not be fraud, but I won't have to do as much.'"

Colleges have largely responded by devoting more resources to academic support services. They are hiring more tutors, building new academic centers and beefing up compliance offices.

If more academic fraud cases have surfaced in recent years, it's most likely a product of better reporting and more collaboration among those monitoring the athletics departments, said Phil Hughes, associate director of athletics for student services at Kansas State University and president of the National Association of Academic Advisors for Athletes.

Academic Support Groups Need More Support

Hughes said he understands the increasing demands on athletics and academic support employees, who are spending more time tracking real-time data for the Academic Progress

Rate (the NCAA's primary new way of measuring athletes' and teams' classroom progress) and helping struggling students, which can take time away from helping other students, athlete or non.

Barker, the Clemson president, said he typically doesn't meet with the academic support staff who provides tutoring and other services to the general study body (as opposed to athletes) because he doesn't see the pressures of committing academic misconduct there to be as great.

At Clemson, both academic support offices report to the university's provost. Some have called for more colleges to remove the perceived wall between athletics and the rest of the academy by moving tutors assigned to athletes into academic affairs, or at least providing students and athletes with the same degree of academic support.

Hughes sees reason for optimism in the academic support landscape: Advisers who once felt like they worked directly for the football coach are increasingly reporting that they feel insulated from that pressure, he said.

Holland, the East Carolina athletics director, said that simply adding more tutors doesn't get at the problem. Colleges still face the risk of having lower-level employees (often graduate students) making important judgment calls about what the proper boundaries are in helping a student stay eligible. The NCAA, he added, is also complicit in adding stress to the academic support system by scheduling events during busy test periods instead of moving more contests to the weekend.

"It Comes Down to Trust"

But Tomas Jimenez, executive director of the LSU Academic Center for Student Athletes, said he isn't convinced that entering students are any less prepared than before, or that the NCAA's new academic rules are leading to more cases of academic misconduct.

"It's always easy to point the finger at the NCAA, but it takes institutions to step up for academic support," he said.

Goldfield, the Charlotte professor, said he doesn't entirely blame athletics departments for misconduct, either. Faculty are often guilty of grade manufacturing or taking part in schemes in which athletes are funneled to their class and largely given a pass.

And what about the role of students in such scandals? Kerry Kenny, vice-chair of the Division I Student-Athlete Advisory Committee, which represents the interests of athletes in the NCAA's top competitive level, said that while it's unfair to judge all athletes by the actions of a few, the group as a whole needs to make better decisions about how it uses help from academic support employees.

In the end, most agree it comes down to trust.

"We have to rely on the integrity of the people involved," Goldfield said.

> *"College athletics is not for everyone, and many student athletes can't cut it, so pay the players! Pay them something for all their time and their efforts!"*

College Athletes Should Be Paid

Al Woods

Al Woods, a professional college recruiter, asserts in the following viewpoint that college sports produce millions of dollars for the schools and coaches, yet the players who do most of the work do not share in the profit. He argues that the players often put so much effort into their sport that their academics suffer; some even give up education altogether. Woods further maintains that many athletes are being paid surreptitiously; therefore, paying them a salary would end much of the corruption that occurs in athletic programs today.

As you read, consider the following questions:

1. According to Al Woods, why do players accept money and other items from colleges in secret?

2. What is the main focus of college athletic programs, according to Woods?

Al Woods, "Should College Athletes Be Paid?" EzineArticles.com, October 30, 2007. Reproduced by permission.

3. If high school players sign a contract and accept money from a professional team, can they change their minds and play for a college team at a later time?

College sports bring in big dollars every year on the major college level. These programs bring $30 [million] and sometimes $40 million dollars per year to the universities and colleges and the players get nothing. These are the same players who are breaking their backs for the university day in and day out and can't get a share of that money and, to me, that does not seem fair. I know what you may be thinking: that these student athletes are getting a free education or have gotten a scholarship to play ball at that university. To me, that's the least they could be doing.

When I look at college football on Saturdays and see packed stadiums with cheering fans paying big money for a ticket I say, what business out there could run a company and not pay its workers? You would think I was talking about some Third World country! Pay the players now, please!

Think about this one: most of the college coaches get six figure salaries—big college coaches get shoe contracts, some get T.V. and radio contracts and many other perks along the way. Also, if they are good coaches and win games they will be offered another coaching job somewhere else with bigger money and larger perks! The student athletes get nothing and, to me, something should be done about that. Please pay the players now!

Some Athletes Are Getting Paid Under the Table

They will keep telling you that the athletes are getting the free education, free books, free room and board and the chance at a good college education that will last a lifetime. So what! Pay the players! I see this whole college thing as slave-labor! Coaches make big money on the backs of these players. You hear stories about college athletes taking money or getting paid under the table. You hear these stories of players getting cars and lots of cash, you hear stories of players getting all of this and more on the side. You hear about the player's families getting cars and houses to attend that college program. This goes on all the time in secret!

Why do the players take this money and cars and houses for their families and much more? Well one reason is recruiting; some college programs feel that in order to get a major college recruit they have to offer these things. Some college programs (not all) have to give something to get these kids. Some of these players come from poor backgrounds, so for these kids to get some money is a big deal especially if the players and their families don't have money anyway.

College Athletes Work Hard

Being a college athlete is very hard. In the first place the amount of hours that these players put in is a lot—every day of every week. They are in class all day, then there's practice after practice, they go eat dinner if they can and then go study. Now all of this may sound simple to you but the amount of time these student athletes are putting in is huge. Then the coaches want more. There could be film to study and there could be times when they are being seen by the athletic trainer. As a student athlete, you have to focus on your studies and your athletic performance or they will try to get rid of you.

College athletics is hard. Sometimes at the end of the day you are exhausted and don't feel like studying or if they have some kind of study table for the players you may not be able to totally focus and, oftentimes, your attention is elsewhere. Just think about the millions of people who go to work every day. They work long hours and may have long commutes to and from home. I'm sure the last thing working people want to do is spend extra hours doing more work. Most working people want to relax, maybe have a beer and watch some T.V. then call it a day. The big difference is they are getting paid for the service and time, and college ball players are not.

Most of the college student athletes do not get their college degrees, and one reason is the workouts and the games that they play. There is so much pressure to do well that something will fall off and that something is their education. College coaches have been known to look the other way as it relates to student athletes and their academics as long as that player can help win games.

For most college athletes, when their eligibility is used up the college programs have no more need for their services. Why would they? For 4 years these college programs have worked these young men and women to death every day. The college programs have gotten all that they could get out of these players and then some. At the college level or at any level it's only about winning games and bringing in big money.

Some Athletes Give Up Education

Take a look at baseball; if a high school baseball player is really good, he can be offered a contract to sign with a major league baseball team. Sometimes the offer is $200,000 and, I've heard, as much as $2 million dollars. Now if that high school baseball player takes that money, they forfeit their college eligibility. Some high school baseball players pass on the money to attend college where they can get better, sharpen their baseball skills and be drafted again by a major league team. Many high school baseball players take the money and take the chance to try and make it in the major leagues. A great many players never make it to the majors. Some play in the minor leagues for years until they realize that their dream of playing in the majors is not going to happen and they move on to something else.

Once you take that money you can't go back and try to play college baseball. The same is true for all the other sports.

From a College Athlete's Perspective

There is no question about it—college athletes are fortunate. We have been given an opportunity to get an education while playing sports that we enjoy.

However. . .

Just because we are fortunate does not mean that we should not try to minimize risks and secure basic protections.

The NCAA tries to convince us that we have little, if anything, to complain about because we are getting a "free ride" through college. This is not true. Our scholarships are not free—we WORK for them.

The following explains how college athletes EARN an opportunity to get a college education:

- Year-round strength and conditioning workouts.

- Countless hours per week of mandatory participation in a sport (hours per week greatly increase because "voluntary" activities are performed).

- Injuries and surgeries that are endured throughout an athlete's career.

- Risk of permanent physical disability and death.

- Generating billions of dollars from TV contracts, ticket sales, etc.

- Giving national exposure to our schools.

College athletes do not get a "free ride." Our education definitely has a price. Hard work and high risks are the trade-off for our scholarships. We should not have to keep quiet while being subjected to unethical conditions.

National College Players Association, 2008.

You'll have high school basketball players trying to make it to the NBA; you have young men try out for the NFL. Many of these athletes never gave education a chance, and many who are in college never got their degree.

College athletes struggle with their academics. Many do not graduate and some just quit altogether. College athletics is not for everyone, and many student athletes can't cut it, so pay the players! Pay them something for all their time and their efforts!

Schools Should Share the Wealth with the Workers

When these college programs are playing in bowl games and making millions on the backs of the players and the players get nothing still, that's wrong. When its "March Madness" time for college basketball and millions are glued to the T.V. every day for hours and the players are giving their all—they still get nothing!

Why would it be a problem to pay players? The schools are making millions of dollars anyway. This is not Mexico or China where the workers are getting paid $1.00 per hour to make billions for some corporation—you know slave labor!

Why do you think players take money from many outside sources? Why do players get suspended from the team for breaking team rules? Why are college programs put on probation? It's all because of money. You have many players coming from disadvantaged backgrounds where there is no money in their families. If these disadvantaged young student athletes had to pay for college out of their own pockets, most would not be in a college at all.

Some student athletes come from backgrounds where the educational system is not that good. Their school districts are under-funded and mismanaged. For many student athletes, their way out is an education with the full athletic scholarships. Playing a sport is their future. Many student athletes only focus on athletics thinking that one day they will be good enough to play in the pros. So when money is dangled in front of the faces of some student athletes, the temptation has to be overwhelming!

For a great many years we have heard stories of players and coaches getting in trouble because of money. We've heard of situations of entire college programs being killed off by the NCAA [National Collegiate Athletic Association] because of money being given to players. Why do they do it? Why is money a problem? One reason is because it's easy to get certain types of players from certain kinds of backgrounds. Big-time college programs can only survive with big-time major college players, so they pay them. We all know that paying college athletes is wrong (set by the guidelines of the NCAA). But this rule needs to change now.

Paying Athletes Would Solve Many Problems

If college athletes are getting scholarships, then they can be paid. If players are getting paid, then I believe you would have more college athletes graduate from college because there would be a stronger incentive to work hard in the classroom. Larger universities pay college coaches more based on their performance, and the players should get paid as well.

If the players are getting paid, then this corruption would stop. No more booster paying players, no more college players selling their shoes, no more college players taking jobs that pay them big money just to work a few hours. It's hard out there for a student athlete! Did you know that a non-student athlete can get a job to earn extra money and can work around their schedules but a student athlete can't have a job until the school year is over, and there are restrictions as to the type of job they can have?

In the game of college athletics, the rules are not fair for the college student athletes! The playing field is not equal. Pay the players!

> "The main problem with paying student athletes is that it is not the college's primary function. The primary function of academic institutions is to educate."

College Athletes Should Not Be Paid

Krikor Meshefejian

In the following viewpoint, Krikor Meshefejian acknowledges the valid points offered from both sides of the "pay athletes to play" debate. But the author maintains that the primary function of colleges and universities is to provide an education for students—not to "hire" students for their athletic contributions. However, Meshefejian does admit that the current athletic scholarship programs need to be reformed to cover full tuition and cost-of-living expenses, and he asserts that such policy changes would help prevent violations of the National Collegiate Athletic Association rules. Krikor Meshefejian was the sports editor for The Illinois Business Law Journal *from 2005 through 2007.*

Krikor Meshefejian, "Pay to Play: Should College Athletes Be Paid?" *The Illinois Business Law Journal*, March 23, 2005. Reproduced by permission.

As you read, consider the following questions:

1. According to Krikor Meshefejian, would paying athletes to play result in increased competition among college teams?
2. What is the benefit that colleges already provide student athletes, according to the author?
3. If they currently do not, what should academic institutions always provide their student athletes, according to Meshefejian?

Does it make sense for an academic institution to run a multimillion dollar entertainment business, which is what college football and college basketball have become? Does it make sense for these institutions to pay the student-athletes who participate in these football and basketball programs?

The reality is that college sports programs, namely the "big name" programs such as football and basketball programs at marquee schools, are businesses that stand to make a large amount of money for their respective schools. According to an article in the *Harvard Journal on Legislation*, "[i]n the past twelve years, the amount of money generated by these two sports has increased nearly 300%, such that they now fund almost all other sports programs." The student-athletes who participate in these programs are part of the reason why these schools stand to make such handsome profits: through ticket sales, endorsement deals, broadcasting deals, and jersey sales (although player names cannot be represented on jerseys), among other things.

The Debate from Both Sides

Mark Murphy, Director of Athletics at Northwestern University, who participated in an ESPN [sports television channel] debate on the topic of paying student-athletes, argues that these athletes currently receive scholarships, whose value, in some instances, totals close to $200,000 over four years. He

Misuse of Athletic Scholarships

During the past four decades, the NCAA [National Collegiate Athletic Association] has crafted a payment system that provides a relatively cheap and steady supply of blue-chip athletes for the burgeoning business of collegiate sports and gives coaches the kind of control over them that employers have over employees. It is little wonder that a recent survey of college athletes by the NCAA found that the majority of those polled identify themselves more as athletes than as students.

Allen Sack, "Should College Athletes Be Paid?"
Christian Science Monitor, March 7, 2008.

stated that all student-athletes have made similar commitments to the schools, and that football and basketball players should not be treated any different than other athletes, who participate in sports that are not as popular and lucrative. Paying athletes anything beyond a scholarship, argues Murphy, would cause problems, particularly from a gender equity standpoint. What Murphy seems to refer to when he says "gender equity" is Title IX federal regulations, which cut off federal funding of colleges if those colleges discriminate on the basis of sex. Paying male student-athletes more than female student-athletes could possibly be construed as discrimination.

However, others argue that these athletes are producing revenues not only for the schools, which give these students scholarships, but also for shoe companies, television networks, and the conference in which these schools belong. Moreover, the equity problem could obviously be solved if all collegiate athletes get paid the same base salary for their participation.

There are also student-athletes who have to leave school early because they do not have enough money to continue or to pay their bills, and leaving school for a career in professional sports is an easy way of making money. The argument is that if student-athletes get paid, they will remain in school and complete their education.

The Payment System Is Problematic

But, is money such a big problem for these student-athletes? Don't they receive scholarships? How much more money do they need? The truth is that "full" scholarships do not always entirely cover tuition and cost of living. However, these students can still do what a majority of students do, which is to get loans. Still, some of these student-athletes do not qualify for such loans, so there is still a gap between the money they get and the total cost of attendance. This gap coupled with the fact that football and basketball players help generate so much revenue, has caused some intercollegiate teams to provide their athletes with extra compensation, which is in direct violation of NCAA [National Collegiate Athletic Association] by-laws.

Perhaps creating a method of payment above and beyond scholarships would help to decrease the amount of corruption, and "under the table" activities of some of these nationally recognized sports programs. But creating such a system may also lead to other problems. Developing such an economy in college football and basketball would result in a monetary race to buy the best athletes in the country. This would lead to a significant gap in talent between rich schools and poor schools. The disparity would result in a lack of competition, and may result in "Cinderella" teams becoming a thing of the past. The more the disparity, the less the competition, and the less the competition, the less excitement. Less excitement will result in less revenue, and less revenue means less money for collegiate programs other than basketball and football. Ultimately, however, the main concern with paying athletes should not be one of establishing competitive balance and preserving "Cinderella" teams.

The College Experience Is Payment Enough

The main problem with paying student-athletes is that it is not the college's primary function. The primary function of academic institutions is to educate, and not to hire student-athletes for their contributions on the basketball court or football field. Moreover, colleges already provide student-athletes with an invaluable benefit. This benefit comes in the form of a college degree, which gives students opportunities in the job market that they would otherwise not have had. These basketball and football programs also provide some student-athletes the opportunity to get excellent educations for which they normally would not have been qualified, or have applied. These programs also give student-athletes the opportunity to become professional athletes. Moreover, most of these sports programs have been around long before present-day student-athletes began to participate in them. How much of the financial success can be attributed to the players, especially in college sports, where a team's success is largely dependent on the coach's and his or her staff's abilities?

Many of these programs were profitable long before some of these players arrived, and some of these players probably chose a particular program because of their past success. These players may have chosen a school due to the amount of scholarship money they were receiving, but scholarship money is usually not enough to overwhelm other considerations such as a school's academic standing, the coach's leadership and teaching skills, and a school's reputation. Paying student-athletes any more than a scholarship would put such considerations in jeopardy, resulting in student's making decisions based on how much money they are offered, as opposed to making decisions based on where they will succeed in all aspects of college life. The college experience, a student-athlete's educational experience should be about more than just dollars and cents.

Athletic Scholarship Reform

Despite the strength of the reasons as to why student-athletes should not be paid, there are certain problems with the current NCAA system which can and should be cured. The gap between a full scholarship and the cost of attendance should be covered by the academic institution, especially when a student-athlete does not qualify for a loan. Such a policy will go a long way in ensuring that student-athletes are not leaving school to become professional athletes because they cannot pay their bills. Academic institutions should be able to provide at least that much for their athletes. Ultimately, this is a form of payment, but it is not the type of payment that some individuals are advocating. The primary purpose of these institutions is to educate; it is the coach's job to teach, and not just in terms of the sport a student athlete plays. These schools should facilitate the educations of student-athletes through scholarship grants, but not through a system of salaries dependent on supply and demand, which ultimately [deters]. . .a student-athlete from picking a school, and [deters]. . .them from attending a school, for the right reasons.

| "Student-athletes thus must be both students and athletes, including in how they are recruited and admitted."

College Athletic Recruiting Should Be Reformed

Institute of Higher Education, University of Georgia

In the following viewpoint, the authors from the Institute of Higher Education contend that the college athletic recruiting process needs to be reformed because student athletes too often come to college unprepared and even uninterested in academics. They suggest that those in the athletic departments should work together with their schools' academic administrators throughout the entire admissions process to enhance a mutual understanding and interest in the success of both programs. Founded in 1964, the Institute of Higher Education's mission is to improve postsecondary education policy and practice.

As you read, consider the following questions:

1. The authors maintain that the recruitment and admission of student-athletes must be grounded in what principles?

"Athletics Recruiting and Academic Values: Enhancing Transparency, Spreading Risk, and Improving Practice," Institute of Higher Education, University of Georgia, Fall 2006. Reproduced by permission. This project was supported by grants from the Knight Foundation and the University of Georgia President's Venture Fund.

2. Do the authors believe that college athletics can be re-formed to be free from commercialism and professionalism?

3. According to the authors, should student athletes arrive in school before their first term begins so they can learn such things as team-building as an athlete?

In late August [2006], the Institute of Higher Education at the University of Georgia assembled 20 presidents, athletics directors, campus and conference administrators, and leading scholars writing on intercollegiate athletics for a day-long discussion of the challenges associated with athletics recruiting. The roundtable focused on framing issues in recruiting student-athletes in the context of the entire university. We worked from the prospect that trends and challenges across higher education parallel and thus can inform and be informed by those in intercollegiate athletics, concluding that positive change in areas such as athletics recruiting cannot occur if it is considered in isolation from the whole of university communities. The recruitment and admission of student-athletes must be grounded in the principles of academe—and it must involve faculty and academic administrators in meaningful ways.

We thus explore the athletics recruiting and admissions process with a view toward reconceptualizing it, advancing an approach that improves practice through spreading the risks associated with recruiting and admissions across universities as a whole by enhancing transparency in the process. By more formally and completely involving the entire university community in recruiting student-athletes, we suggest a means of counterbalancing the negative incentives and poor decisions that too often define what fundamentally must be a legitimate admissions process.

A Needless Divide

Academic administrators and faculty members must be involved directly in the recruiting process from beginning to end. Such an approach will move them beyond the stereotypes and vague laments that so many believe about college sports, perhaps even toward welcoming—and even taking credit for—competitive successes by athletes who are also bona fide students. Meanwhile, it requires those in athletics to work transparently within the university. They must internalize academic values, embracing them even when inconvenient, if they are to retain the mantle of education that distinguishes college sports from purely professional endeavors.

Troubles associated with recruiting are attributable to the divide that has long been perceived between academics and athletics—a divide that not only is unnecessary but also is counterproductive and even dangerous for institutions. . . .

The crises in athletics that can prove burdensome to university administrations are often attributable to a failure by athletics to comprehend the values and mores of academic life. Similarly, colleagues in academe must come to understand the realities of contemporary intercollegiate athletics, and recognize that calls for reform in areas like recruiting must be realistic. Just as "turning back the clock" to a time of abundant state subsidies to institutions with little demand for accountability is unrealistic, so is restoring athletics to some golden age that never existed free from commercialism and professionalism.

The values asserted in discussing reform in intercollegiate athletics must acknowledge the commercial contexts in which institutions as a whole operate—that athletics at large universities are consistent with how these institutions engage in several other activities that are expected to generate revenue. Such activities must also be grounded in academic values, of course. Student-athletes thus must be both students and athletes, including in how they are recruited and admitted. Building the understanding of academic values needed by those in athletics, and the appreciation of contexts in athletics by those in academe, requires structural and cultural means to encourage regular interaction between the two. . . .

Operating in a Vacuum

Why are athletes and coaches so often making poor judgments that lead to familiar headlines about embarrassingly low retention rates and a class of students divorced from institutional life apart from their role as athletes? The answer is usually that the recruitment and admission of student-athletes occurs in a vacuum, with coaches and prospective student-athletes making decisions without needed involvement of faculty, academic administrators, or even campus admissions officers.

Coaches are forced to work within a deeply flawed system with increasingly high stakes. They are limited by well meaning NCAA [National Collegiate Athletic Association] rules in the contacts they can have with recruited athletes and thus the information they can provide to guide them to a good decision. Recruited athletes too often choose an institution with only a vague awareness of not only the approach of their soon-to-be coach and nature of his or her team, but also the academic and social environment on campus. For instance, the summer recruiting tournaments, which were created in response to rules imposed to prevent basketball coaches from becoming nuisances to the most desirable recruits, require that coaches watch from the bleachers and not interact directly with the athletes. Thus they lose the opportunity to provide the good counsel that is critical in any admissions process—a classic unintended consequence of rulemaking by member institutions rightly acting to temper undue competitive pressures.

Furthermore, recruiting has become a fixation for coaches. They identify prospective athletes early in high school (or even before then), communicating with them obsessively.

NCAA rules limiting such contact are subject to loopholes that are exploited, as with coaches discovering text messaging as a means around restrictions on telephone calls or sending e-mail messages. Recruited athletes are receiving these contacts well before they set foot on a campus and are aware of the challenges associated with attending a university or college.

It only heightens the challenges that coaches have strong incentives to have athletes commit to attending an institution as early as possible, often on the first day of contact the NCAA permits between coaches and athletes. Recruited athletes can thus experience a truncated admissions process, shortchanging the usual process by which students get to know institutions (and themselves) and institutions get to know them before committing to one another. Both are assuming significant risk without exercising sufficient due diligence. . . .

Ensuring integrity in the recruiting process then is less a matter of applying more rules and much more an issue of ensuring that values are clarified and applied. The only reasonable way to do so is through the transparency that comes with involving the entire academic community in the recruiting process.

Institutions effectively ask coaches alone to paint a picture of what life as a college student at their institution will be like. Thus when these recruited athletes arrive on campus, especially in the spectator sports, their impressions of the university have often been shaped only by the one football or basketball game weekend on which they made a recruiting visit, plus constant but long distance communications with coaches. They may have little, if any, sense of the realities of managing a full load of courses while practicing, traveling, and competing. And they may have had only cursory, if any, contact with faculty members, "regular" admissions counselors and academic advisors, or even students other than those associated with teams.

Coaches, then, expect academic advisors employed by athletics departments to pick up the pieces once they arrive, teaching athletes, as best they can, to be college students. What results from the vacuum in recruiting and the differences in preparation between recruits and other freshmen is that athletes are increasingly disconnected from other students. . . .

Serving Underrepresented Students

It is important to remember that the majority of student athletes are not underprepared for higher education. But low-achieving students from marginal, under-resourced high schools rarely matriculate at flagship universities unless they happen to be athletes. Many blue-chip athletes come from white-chip backgrounds, from low-income areas and inner city high schools that continue to struggle to prepare students for postsecondary education. Meanwhile, NCAA eligibility standards, with the best of intentions, have moved from standardized tests (which may, in fact, be problematic due to socioeconomic bias) to high school grades and core courses, making it more difficult to identify at-risk students, and opening the door to the kind of fraud seen in the diploma mill scandal.

Student-athletes recruited for the spectator sports also are predominantly African-Americans entering a university environment primarily shaped and populated by whites. Roughly one-quarter of Division I scholarship athletes—and an even higher proportion in the spectator sports (over one-half)—are African-American, compared to about one-tenth of students overall at Division I institutions. So, institutions deeply concerned about expanding access and opportunity to underrepresented students might look to athletics as a model. The question then becomes whether these student-athletes, having been admitted, are receiving the experience that they should as students. Are universities and colleges doing right by them?

Make Academic Integrity Part of the Recruiting Process

Somehow, our culture has developed an obsession with the college choices made by a handful of students. Those students are not National Merit Scholars. They are blue-chip high-school athletes, and the frenzy surrounding the process of recruiting them is reaching a fever pitch this week.

On Feb. 8, [2007] newspapers across the country will devote pages and photos to football players in elaborate "Signing Day" ceremonies, which mark the first day players can sign agreements to attend a specific college and receive an athletic scholarship. Rivals.com projects that it will have 75 million page views on Signing Day alone, more than three times the daily average of CNN.com, the most popular online news website. . . .

The recruiting process has moved away from the academic realm of our institutions and into the commercial realm surrounding college sports. From this process, prospects learn that their choice of college is critically important to an ominous mass of spectators and that they themselves are little more than a bundle of statistics neatly packaged into a one- to five-star rating.

This is a trend that should be troubling not only to college presidents, faculty and athletics personnel but also to parents, high school coaches and anyone who cares about the personal development of these students. Colleges need to consider ways to reclaim the recruiting process for higher education and prevent these students from being treated as a commodity.

R. Gerald Turner and Clifton R. Whanton, Jr.,
"Make Academic Integrity Part of Recruiting Process,"
The Miami Herald, *February 4, 2007.*

The same question applies, of course, to all students admitted from underrepresented groups, particularly when admissions criteria incorporate the racial and ethnic balance of an entering class.

Here exists an important opportunity for a regular and deep conversation bridging academe and athletics. Universities have been successful in introducing underrepresented students to academic opportunities through intensive preparatory experiences, such as in-residence academic programs, during the summer prior to the freshman year. Athletics might emulate this approach by having recruited student-athletes learn the realities of being a college student before their first fall semester in environments divorced from their status as athletes. Doing so would be a departure from the common model of using pre-freshman summer school as a chance to begin team-building and the transition only to being an athlete.

Those on the academic side of institutions can similarly learn from the intensive academic advising, often using a "tough love" approach, invested in athletics. These approaches tend to yield dividends. At most institutions, despite lower test scores and high school grades, football and basketball teams have higher graduation rates for African-American players than the overall student body. . . .

An Illustrative Approach

There is no one approach, of course, to realizing the broader and deeper involvement by the entire university or college community in athletics recruiting that will ensure academic values enter into the process from beginning to end. But every institution can find a structure that will be effective within its own organizational culture and regular academic and admissions processes.

One potential model to consider is currently in use at the University of Oklahoma. For the past four years, the athletics department has invited an academic review committee to consider the application of every marginal, or at-risk, recruited athlete. The committee consists of the senior associate athletics director, who also reports to the provost, as well as the faculty athletics representative and several other faculty members named through the faculty senate. The committee has the authority to interview anyone involved in the recruiting of any student-athlete, usually choosing the head coach of the team involved. The coach must offer an acceptable justification for admitting the recruit and, at least in theory, the conversation happens well in advance of the national signing date for the sport in question.

The committee rarely rejects prospects. What matters is that the process itself brings sunshine to recruiting and forces consideration of the relevant issues in admitting a student-athlete by both coaches and the faculty involved. The approach compels coaches to consider whether each athlete he or she recruits is a good fit for the institution, highlighting potential conflicts early and avoiding certain challenging decisions as coaches drop the most marginal cases from consideration.

Meanwhile, faculty come to know the depth of review undertaken by the coaches into the background of recruited athletes and appreciate the art involved in interpreting transcripts, particularly for prospective students from disadvantaged backgrounds. They also bring their expertise to bear on the ultimate question in recruiting and admissions: what constitutes an acceptable gap between the academic preparation of recruited athletes versus other students. Another advantage is that faculty members and academic administrators educate coaches about the academic demands athletes will confront once enrolled, thus creating an important dialogue about the kind of athlete who can succeed best at a given university or college.

By involving faculty in meaningful ways in the recruiting process, the university is thus encouraging a common set of values and practices, moving athletics toward academic values and academe toward a more realistic outlook. In doing so, the impulse to cut corners is lessened. The same is true integrating athletics recruiting into the overall admissions process of institutions, thus reinforcing the idea that athletes are being recruited to a university and not to a coach or program, while providing opportunities to educate parents and students about the opportunities and responsibilities they will encounter on campus. . . .

The Culture of Youth Sports

Beyond college campuses, and more difficult to address, is the fact that the culture of youth sports is increasingly problematic. Youth sports are becoming more and more commercialized and parental pressure and investment in a child getting a scholarship has never been greater. The dominant signals to these children are that sports are more important than academic preparation—academics require only the attention needed to remain eligible to compete.

There is also a divide that increasingly occurs between athletes and others, a notion that athletes are special, subject to different rules from their peers and exempt from normal requirements. The recruiting process only intensifies this perception, thanks to the need coaches feel to court athletes so intensively and even sycophantically [winning the favor of athletes through flattery]. Elite athletes come to thus expect the recruiting process to extend into their time in college, do not take school seriously in high school, and come to college unprepared magnifying the disadvantages they already face. There is clearly a need for a national discussion of how to better communicate the realities of academe to the youth sports culture.

"Is it possible to restructure organized competitive sports to make them good for America?... It appears government intervention is now the only way to bring about requisite reform."

College Athletic Recruiting Needs Government Intervention

Frank G. Splitt

In the following viewpoint, Frank G. Splitt contends that the unrestrained commercialization of college sports is undermining American educational values that are essential for the nation's economic and physical well-being. Splitt further maintains that because the National Collegiate Athletic Association (NCAA) will not on its own make the reforms necessary to restore academic integrity to the collegiate environment, the government should intervene to bring about the requisite reform. Frank G. Splitt holds a Ph.D. in electrical and computer engineering and has written several essays on college sports reform.

Frank G. Splitt, "Are Big-Time College Sports Good for America?" thedrakegroup.org, January 2006. Reproduced by permission. http://thedrakegroup.org/Splitt_Good _for_America.pdf.

As you read, consider the following questions:

1. According to Frank G. Splitt, how does the NCAA help the National Football League and the National Basketball Association?

2. What is the NCAA's strategy to maintain its big business without government intervention, according to Splitt?

3. Does the author believe that high school sports are managing to stay relatively free of the commercial excesses found in college sports?

The negative impact of college sports on higher education is not a new story. In 1929, the *Chicago Tribune* featured a headline column on the Carnegie Report's indictment of college sports. This report focused on the need for reform based on the negative influence of big-time college sports on higher education—stating that:

> "(College football) is not a student's game as it once was. It is a highly organized commercial enterprise. The athletes who take part in it have come up through years of training; they are commanded by professional coaches; little if any initiative of ordinary play is left to the player. The great matches are highly profitable enterprises. Sometimes the profits go to finance college sports, sometimes to pay the cost of the sports amphitheater, in some cases the college authorities take a slice for college buildings."

The Ruination of College Sports

Some seven years after publication of the *Chicago Tribune* story, Paul Gallico gave up a successful sports-writing career with the *New York Daily News* to devote himself to full-time writing. His first book was *Farewell to Sport*, published in 1938. As the title suggests, it was his farewell to sports writing, but it was much more than a farewell. It illuminated the increasing professionalism in sports during the 1930s, and bemoaned the loss of sport in its original sense. The following 68-year-old Gallico quotes provide additional context for this essay:

> "College football today is one of the last great strongholds of genuine old-fashioned American hypocrisy.... There are occasionally abortive attempts to turn football into an honest woman, but, to date, the fine old game that interests and entertains literally millions of people has managed to withstand these insidious attacks.... It is a curious thing that the college to which a boy goes, not only for an education, but for the set of morals, ethics, and ideals with which to carry on in later life, is the first place he learns beyond any question of doubt that you can get away with murder if you don't get caught at it or if you know the right people when you do get nabbed. His university is playing a dirty, lying game and it doesn't take him long to find out.... If there is anything good about college football it is the fact that it seems to bring entertainment, distraction, and pleasure to many millions of people. But the price, the sacrifice to decency, I maintain is too high."

Robert Maynard Hutchins, President of the University of Chicago and a contemporary of Gallico, deplored undue emphasis on nonacademic pursuits. Guided by his personal beliefs and, perhaps, triggered by Gallico's remarks, he abolished football at the University of Chicago in 1939. When asked why he did this he replied with the simple statement ["To be successful, one must cheat. Everyone is cheating, and I refuse to cheat."] As former Tufts University Provost Sol Gittleman opined "A Robert Hutchins comes only once in a lifetime."

In his 2002 book, *SPORTS—The All-American Addiction*, John Gerdy argues that our society's huge investment in organized sports is unjustified, claiming that ardent boosters say that sports embody the "American Way"—developing winners by teaching lessons in sportsmanship, teamwork, and discipline.

I concur with Gerdy's claims that America's obsession with modern sports is eroding American life and undermining traditional American values essential to the well-being of the nation and its people—allowing Americans to escape problems and ignore issues as if they were drug addicts.

Gerdy asks tough questions. Have sports lost their relevance? Is it just mindless entertainment? Is our enormous investment in sports as educational tools appropriate for a nation that needs graduates to compete in the information-based, global economy of the twenty-first century? Do organized sports continue to promote positive ideals? Or, do sports, in the age of television, corporate skyboxes, and sneaker deals, represent something far different?. . .

In Need of Reform

To begin, college sports are big business, and the NCAA [National Collegiate Athletic Association] is not in the business of reform. The NCAA is in the business of staying in business as the franchiser of professional-caliber, big-time college-sports programs for its member school franchisees. Together with the schools, the NCAA exploits college athletes while making huge amounts of tax-exempt money under the guise of an institution of higher education. In effect, the government-subsidized NCAA manages minor league teams for the NFL [National Football League] and the NBA [National Basketball Association]—supplying a stream of professional-level athletes for their respective drafts.

The NCAA's strategy to stay in business is to maintain the illusion that they are an institution of higher education, that college athletes are really students on a legitimate degree-seeking track, and that it is capable of instituting requisite reforms without government intervention and a consequent loss of its tax-exempt status.

Hiring Myles Brand [president of the NCAA] was a key tactic—providing him with a total annual compensation in the order of $1 million to allow him to live large along with the NCAA's top brass while he gives the NCAA an academic front. Brand was not empowered by the NCAA to initiate serious reform, i.e., to emulate Judge Kenesaw Mountain Landis, baseball's first commissioner who was able to take firm control of major league baseball when its integrity was in question. Simply stated, the NCAA would never allow Brand to accomplish serious reform.

Other NCAA anti-reform tactics are to co-opt external reform efforts by "working together," to provide weak rules enforcement, and to shroud its nefarious conduct in a veil of secrecy—protected by the Buckley Amendment to the Family Educational Rights and Privacy Act—operating as the least transparent business in America. . . .

The key facts are these: there is no one charged with anything resembling responsibility for controlling the wretched excesses of big-time college sports; the NCAA has become expert at resisting true reform and co-opting would-be, well-intentioned reform initiatives; few, if any, college presidents can buck the system today and expect to keep their jobs; faculty members, even though protected by tenure, have little chance of making any real impact internally; and sadly, high school sports are becoming just as corroded as they are at the college and professional levels. Also, if a school with a big-time athletics program should decide to cut it back, it would be faced with the almost impossible job of replacing the revenues to service the large debt on its athletics facilities; not every school has billionaire boosters that can donate $165 million to its athletics fund or provide major gifts for athletic facilities.

This is a bleak situation indeed—prompting one of the reviewers of this essay to comment that it brought to mind the near-impossible predicaments the British created over time by importing Protestants to Northern Ireland in the 17th century and by carving up the Ottoman Empire after World War I to form, among other things, Iraq. Some even say this is a lost cause.

Possibility of Restructuring

The obvious question is: What, if anything, can be done? Is it possible to restructure organized competitive sports to make them good for America? I believe that the answer is yes. However, as painful as it may be, it appears government intervention is now the only way to bring about requisite reform.

One way the government could intervene to clean up big-time college sports is to employ the quid pro quo (no reform-no tax exemption) strategy outlined in "What Congress Can Do About the Mess in College Sports" [written by Frank G. Splitt]. Implementation of this strategy would help bring about academic and financial disclosure and the restoration of academic and financial integrity in America's institutions of higher learning. Failure to implement and comply with congressionally-stipulated corrective measures over a reasonable amount of time would put the NCAA and/or individual institutions at risk of losing their nonprofit status. Once implemented, evidence of a continuation of existing patterns of fraud, continued efforts by universities and colleges to circumvent the intent of the reform measures, or, retaliation against whistleblowers, would garner penalties of such severity as to make the risk of noncompliance not even worth thinking about. However, since schools would still be saddled with the burdens and temptations associated with the college-sports entertainment business, even more radical approaches may prove to be necessary in the light of new global realities.

These approaches would involve divestiture—the elimination of professional-level sports from America's education system. This would not only put a long overdue end to the NCAA's contrived façade of 'amateurism' but also release the

Questioning the Tax-Exempt Status

College sports are so scandal rife, herculean muscle must be applied just to compile a list of recent NCAA [National Collegiate Athletic Association] scandals.... NCAA athletes and coaches, even professors who cater to college athletes, have industriously devised all manner of venality to further the cause of victory for home teams. There are all sorts of scandals: hazing, sex scandals, grades, recruitment, point shaving, and game fixing. Throw in gambling and rape, and you haven't even begun to list them all.

No wonder, then, that Congress should start thinking about pulling this multibillion-dollar business's inappropriate tax-exempt status. Outgoing House Ways and Means Committee Chair Bill Thomas ... queried the NCAA in letter form about how executives justify nonprofit status while raking in billions of dollars in TV revenue for game broadcasts, paying coaches exorbitant salaries, negotiating massive corporate sponsorships, and maintaining straight-facedly that they are "further[ing] the educational purpose of Division I-A schools."

"Educational purpose" is the bootstrap NCAA football and basketball teams use to share in their colleges' and universities' nonprofit status. But it's one that has vastly outlived its original purpose and is hollering to be yanked....

Why in this day and age do American taxpayers continue to subsidize a mammoth, profit-rich industry? Let's hope Thomas's successor agrees that there's no valid reason any longer.

Bonnie Erbe, "End the Scandal-Plagued NCAA's Tax Exemption,"
U.S. News & World Report, *November 6, 2006.*

stranglehold the college-sports entertainment business has on our institutions of higher learning. . . .

It is to be expected that those who benefit from a continuation of the status quo will continue to resist reforms that pose a threat to their tax-exempt status—railing and retaliating against individuals and organizations that tell the brutal truth about big-time college sports.

Also, if and when, Congressional hearings are called to investigate this blight on America's system of higher education, fierce opposition will be mounted. Resistance will no doubt take the form of a well-organized, well-funded, lobbying and public-relations campaign orchestrated by the NCAA—bringing to bear its financial power and its friends in the media as well as in federal and state governments. In other words, the NCAA would be in a fight for its life using all of its awesome financial and political resources to protect its money making machine.

There will certainly be screams to keep the government out of college sports with claims of grandstanding and posturing by members of Congress—forgetting that it is the government that is subsidizing the growth of the big-time college-sports entertainment business in the first place.

America's Well-Being at Stake

Hopefully, enlightened legislators will see that America can no longer afford to have its educational system, the health of its citizens, and its place in the global economy, undermined by professional-level college sports programs; and, then go on to see the connection between college-sports reform and the National Academies' recommendations set forth in their report, *Rising Above the Gathering Storm*. Subsidizing institutions of higher education so they can serve as centers for public entertainment is not a smart thing to do in today's world.

Big-time college-sports entertainment is embedded in America's culture. The NCAA, with its ability to control the money game and thwart reform, coupled with its ability to exploit America's love affair with sports and its high tolerance for misbehavior by its heroes, has helped bring about a horrific mess in big-time, college sports ... a mess characterized by seemingly unrestrained growth in spending with a corresponding desperate need by "hooked" schools for additional revenues.

The wealth and health of America and its citizens are at risk. Based upon the magnitude of the problems and the high stakes involved, it would seem obvious that government intervention is in our national interest. We can no longer afford the luxury of muddling along with a handicap—engaging in distracting, resource-draining activities that divert our attention from new global realities.

Likewise, reform cannot be deterred by naysayers who would either discount the threat or label reform efforts as an exercise in futility. To succumb to this negativism and do nothing would all but ensure the eventual decline of America's position on the world stage.

There appears to be no option but to respond with resolute intensity, resources, and vigor. Will it happen? Unfortunately, not immediately; perhaps it may never happen at all. There are no guarantees, but we must at least begin. So what is the Congress waiting for?

> *"Coaches are trying to lock down prized recruits as early as possible—even if it means making commitments when the recruits are barely old enough to be prized."*

College Athletic Programs Are Recruiting Middle School Students

Andy Staples

Andy Staples, a columnist for Sports Illustrated, *discloses in the following viewpoint that college coaches are not only looking at high school players as possible recruits, but they also are considering and committing to middle school players. Even though these young prospects have not fully developed physically or emotionally, the competition among sports teams has become so great that college scouts are eager to obtain verbal agreements from thirteen- and fourteen-year-old standouts, according to Staples. He further contends that posting detailed rankings of middle school athletes has become big business.*

As you read, consider the following questions:

1. How soon are coaches allowed to contact student prospects, according to National Collegiate Athletic Association (NCAA) rules?
2. When can a player sign a college scholarship commitment, according to NCAA rules?
3. According to Andy Staples, are there any serious repercussions if a college coach rescinds a verbal commitment made to a middle school athlete?

Michael Avery, a sweet-shooting, 6'4" guard from Thousand Oaks, Calif., picked a high school late last week: He announced on Friday that he'll attend Crespi Carmelite High in Encino. He already knew, however, where he will go to college. On May 1, the 15-year-old Avery—he's finishing up the eighth grade—and his father, Howard, called Kentucky coach Billy Gillispie and accepted the scholarship offer Gillispie had extended three days before. A few years ago, news of Avery's verbal commitment (the earliest he can sign a national letter of intent is November 2011) probably would have appeared in SI [*Sports Illustrated*] as this week's Sign of the Apocalypse. Now, it borders on business as usual.

As Early as Possible

Gillispie has been busy of late. He also received a commitment last week from Greenfield, Ohio, ninth-grader Vinny Zollo—and he's not the first coach to raid the nursery more than once. In '06 USC's [University of Southern California] Tim Floyd landed a commitment from L.A. forward Dwayne Polee Jr. before Polee played a high school game. Last year Floyd accepted a commitment from another middle-schooler: Ryan Boatright, an eighth-grade guard in Aurora, Ill. In '06 and '07, Arizona coach Lute Olson offered scholarships to two players (first Scottsdale, Ariz., guard Matt Carlino; then Bryan, Texas, guard J-Mychal Reese) who were about to enter the eighth grade. Neither player accepted the offer and both remain un-committed, but their reaction is not likely to slow the cradle-robbing. "It's like an arms race," Rivals.com national recruiting analyst Jerry Meyer says. "You've got to offer first."

As the pressure to win increases, and competition for the top prospects grows fiercer, coaches are trying to lock down prized recruits as early as possible—even if it means making commitments when the recruits are barely old enough to be prized. Recruiting the very young can be a complicated process, in which coaches work around NCAA [National Collegiate Athletic Association] rules that forbid contacting prospects until June 15 of the student's sophomore year of high school. Often they communicate with players and their families through middlemen. And it is perfectly legal for prospects and their parents to call coaches or make unofficial visits to campuses. (Howard Avery introduced himself to Gillispie at a tournament in Akron last month and later called the coach to discuss his son's future.) "Should I wait until another school offers and then come in?" Floyd told *Time* after Boatright's commitment. "I can't do that. Because they're going to say, 'Well, you're late.'"

A Leap of Faith

Even though the scholarship commitments are nonbinding—a player can't put his college intentions in writing until November of his senior year of high school—a grade school recruitment is a leap of faith for both sides. If the prospect doesn't develop as expected, the coach, assuming he still has a job when the kid is a senior, can slither out of the agreement before a letter of intent is signed. He might save himself a scholarship, but the damage to his reputation as a recruiter could be irreparable. Coaches are reluctant to explicitly break verbal commitments: In a radio interview last week Gilllspie, who is banned by NCAA rules from discussing specific recruits, said he would honor any scholarship he offers.

Andy Friedman.

Recruits run the risk of tying themselves to a program that looks great when they're 14 but—thanks to a coaching change, roster overhaul or a kid's evolving personality and preferences—might not be so enticing when they're 17. A player who pulls out of his commitment runs the risk of not finding a spot at another school. Still, the allure of an early commitment is strong. Howard Avery, a partner in a Santa Monica, Calif., accounting firm, says he tried to "apply the brakes" after Gillispie made the offer to his son. But the more he thought about it, the less reason he could find to wait. Michael knows Kentucky is a powerhouse and that he wants to play for an elite program. "How many parents of eighth-graders, if they were to be offered a scholarship for their child to get a free education at the college of their choice, would say, 'No, I'll wait until he's a senior to make that decision?'" the elder Avery says. "When that kind of offer comes along, I don't care if the kid's in the third grade, the eighth grade or the 12th grade, you take it."

Steve King, a vice president for a Huntington Beach, Calif., data-management firm, disagrees. In 2003 King's son Taylor became one of the first junior high players to accept a college offer: He committed to UCLA [University of California at Los Angeles] between eighth and ninth grade. Two years later Taylor reopened his recruitment; the 6'6" forward eventually signed with Duke [Durham, NC], and last month he transferred to Villanova [Philadelphia, PA] after a year in Durham. King now says he is sorry he allowed his son to commit so young. He believes that by effectively shielding Taylor from the first two years of the conventional recruiting process, he prevented the boy from getting "a valuable learning experience," even if it might have involved hundreds of phone calls from coaches and reporters. "There is a lot to be said about the process," King says. "It helps these kids take information and make sound decisions. Let's face it. These kids in eighth grade, they aren't making those decisions. The parents are."

Crowded Marketplace

More and more parents will test King's theory. While Rivals.com and Scout.com post detailed rankings of the country's best high school players, Hoop Scoop Online has been ranking sixth-grade prospects for several years. Publisher Clark Francis says he doesn't exactly enjoy passing judgment on the jump shots of kids whose voices have yet to crack, but he understands the middle school rankings have helped him carve out a niche in a crowded marketplace. "That's where the trend is," says Francis, who charges $499 for a one-year subscription to his service. "You have no idea how much interest there is."

So, sports fans, your universe of names and numbers is about to expand still more. The No. 1 prospect in the high school graduating class of 2012? Francis says it's Zach Peters, a 6'8", 220-pound forward who is an eighth-grader in Plano, Texas. The word, via Zach's father, Tim, a tech-firm CEO, is that the boy is simply preparing for high school and is not interested in committing to a college right now. He may mean it too. The only thing certain is that the kid is in the driver's seat, even if he's not old enough to drive.

Periodical Bibliography

The following articles have been selected to supplement the diverse views presented in this chapter.

Associated Press	"NCAA: Athletes Graduate at Better Rate," November 9, 2006.
David Broder	"The Sports World in Foul Territory," *The Cagle Post*, April 11, 2008.
Frank Deford	"In All Fairness, College Athletes Should Be Paid," National Public Radio, January 2, 2008.
Dennis Dodd	"Academic Progress Rate: Numbers Don't Tell the Story," CBSSports.com, May 7, 2007.
Barbara H. Fried	"Punting our Future: College Athletics and Admissions," *Change*, May/June 2007.
Rod Gilmore	"College Football Players Deserve Pay for Play," ESPN.com, January 17, 2007.
Lisa Horne	"Since When Is a College Education Not Good Enough Anymore?" FoxSports.com, February 27, 2008.
John Maher	"Athletes Caught Between Standards," *Austin American-Statesman*, October 29, 2007.
Karen McCaghren	"Athletes vs. Academics: Should College Athletes Be Fined for Skipping Class?" AssociatedContent.com, June 12, 2007.
Aaron Steinberg	"Mr. Brand Goes to Washington: Does the NCAA Deserve Non-Profit Status?" *Reason*, January 4, 2007.
Tim Sullivan	"Mayo May Be Wrong; Inequities Not Right," *San Diego Union-Tribune*, May 17, 2008.
Art Thiel	"College Sports Get Academic Wake-Up Call," *Seattle Post-Intelligencer*, May 9, 2008.

OPPOSING
VIEWPOINTS®
SERIES

CHAPTER 3

Is There Equality in Sports?

Chapter Preface

On Monday, April 7, 2008, the Maryland General Assembly passed the Fitness and Athletics Equity for Students with Disabilities Act, and Governor Martin O'Malley signed it into law. The Act ensures that students with disabilities are provided equal opportunities to participate in physical education and athletic programs, and that schools develop policies and procedures to promote and protect the inclusion of students with disabilities. Furthermore, schools must provide annual reporting to the Maryland State Department of Education detailing their compliance with these requirements. Exceptions can be made, according to the bill, when the inclusion of a student "presents an objective safety risk to the student or to others or fundamentally alters the nature of the school's mainstream physical education or mainstream athletic program." While most experts and advocates for the disabled laud the bill's passage, there are some questions and misgivings regarding its implementation.

The push for the legislation began when wheelchair athlete Tatyana McFadden, a Paralympic medal winner and world record holder, filed suit against Atholton High School in Howard County, Maryland, because she was denied the right to participate in interscholastic track events. In the words of the Women's Sports Foundation's Terri Lakowski, "Just thirty-five years ago [1973], prior to the passage of Title IX, schools were engaging in the same discriminatory treatment toward all female athletes—slamming the doors of opportunity in young girls' faces for no other reason than because they were female. Now, history was repeating itself; the doors of opportunity were being slammed shut in the face of a young, female athlete, but for a different reason—because she has a disability." Schools already must adhere to the Rehabilitation Act and the Americans with Disabilities Act, both of which prohibit discrimination on the basis of disability; however, neither of those statutes provides specific regulations and policy guidelines. Recognizing the problem, the Women's Sports Foundation began working with the Maryland Disability Law Center to introduce more specific legislation, which resulted in the Fitness and Athletics Equity for Students with Disabilities Act.

The challenge now becomes how to implement the legislation. How will kids with disabilities compete against their able-bodied peers? In response, Tommie Storms, of the American Association of Adapted Sports Programs, said, "Is the development and integration of an interscholastic athletic model, inclusive to those with disabilities, a difficult undertaking? Yes. Is it impossible? No. Will it wreak havoc on high school athletics? It hasn't in Georgia or Minnesota, or any of a handful of states offering one or more sports within its schools for those with disabilities." In fact, the Minnesota State High School League has sanctioned state titles in four sports for disabled athletes since 1993. And athletes with amputations are being included on football and wrestling teams; for example, Kyle Maynard, a congenital amputee, competed in the 2004 Georgia high school wrestling championship meets, and Rohan Murphy, born without legs, was a wrestler on the Penn State University team in 2005 and 2006.

The Women's Sports Foundation believes that every child deserves the chance to enjoy sports and it plans to take the issue to other states and to the federal government. Discrimination against individuals with disabilities within school systems is just one issue regarding equality in sports. In the following chapter, the authors discuss other factors related to achieving equality in sports.

"*Hiring Latinos just to make the numbers right is wrong. Hiring qualified individuals is right.... You can't just hire people to fill a lot of these jobs.*"

Diversity in Hiring Should Not Be Mandatory in Professional Baseball

Luke Kohler

Luke Kohler, a sports writer who maintains a sports news and editorial Web site, argues in the following viewpoint that trying to achieve racial and gender equality in Major League Baseball (MLB) is unreasonable. Kohler asserts that the positions of baseball players, coaches, and managers should be earned on the basis of ability and knowledge—not handed out just to fulfill a specified quota.

As you read, consider the following questions:

1. According to Luke Kohler, what is perhaps the main reason the number of black baseball players has diminished in the United States?

2. Which has more black baseball players, according to a study by Boyd Nation: college teams or the major leagues?

3. Why don't many Latino baseball players move into major league managerial positions, according to Kohler?

Major League Baseball [MLB] finally got an 'A' for race for it's diversity in hiring, but the number of black players in the league has fallen once again, reaching the level of just 8.2 percent. This comes from *The 2008 Racial and Gender Report Card: Major League Baseball* by Richard Lapchick [director of the University of Central Florida's Institute for Diversity and Ethics in Sport].

Now, I understand that race is always a sensitive issue. Being white, I'm apparently supposed to stay out of the conversation, but when it comes to leaps of logic and plain old-fashioned stupidity, I cannot stand by silently.

Why Are the Numbers Important?

Yes, the number of black players has fallen to 8.2 percent in Major League Baseball. The percentage of black pitchers is just 3 percent. Is this something that warrants a complaint, an investigation and funding to try to change it?

There are problems with this report, and to understand it and for us to make real progress, they must be called out on it.

The question I have is what is the ideal racial proportions for Major League Baseball? Should the management jobs match society's numbers or baseball's? You cannot have more than 100 percent when you add it all up. White players have remained constant at 58-60 percent of the league. Black players have dropped and Latino players have risen. There is absolutely nothing wrong with this, certainly not to the level that we are being told. Going by the national affirmative action standards is not realistic, and to hold MLB to those numbers is unfair. This is not a typical workplace, and should not be treated like one.

Being a professional baseball player or a coach comes down to two things: baseball skills and baseball knowledge. Many of the jobs that are in professional sports have to do with that sport. Including gender equality in a baseball report card is unfair to the sport. When it comes to non-baseball positions within the franchise, those numbers should be kept completely different. You can't lump all jobs within a franchise together and judge baseball for being fair or unfair.

For the sake of this piece, I'll stick more with the major point of the report, which is that black players have fallen to an all-time low of 8.2 percent of the league. Unfortunately, there is a simple explanation for this, but not necessarily a simple solution.

Why Has the Number of Black Baseball Players Diminished?

Black kids don't play baseball as much as they used to. That is a fact, and if you find it unfortunate, then that's fine. I'd love to see more athletes coming out of inner cities, but in today's world, it's not the most realistic idea. You don't see pick-up baseball and stickball games in U.S. cities these days, but you sure as hell do in Latin America. There are great opportunities in basketball and football that there weren't 40 years ago, as well.

Black kids have found other things to do. You can't force them to play ball, just as you can't with white kids. Five or ten years from now, I'd wager that black and white numbers are down as Latino numbers continue to rise. There are just too many options for kids in America these days, especially when compared to kids from Latin America. For many Latino kids, baseball is their chance out, their chance at making enough money to take care of their family, and at the same time, one of the only things to do.

In many of those countries, you don't have the shopping malls, iPods, skateboard parks, 982 channels on television, televisions, theme parks, the Internet in every room of the house, etc. You play baseball or you work for a living, and you do it by 19 years old.

Now, I know this isn't true for every child in every country in Latin America, and it's a bit of a stereotype, but it's an accurate comparison to the United States more often than not. It's not just black kids that aren't playing ball as much, it's American kids [in general].

Another reason that the black numbers are so low is that black representation in college baseball is even lower than in the big leagues. According to a study by Boyd Nation [provides college baseball statistics on the Web site, Boyds World] (non scientific), only 5.3% of college baseball players in 2005 were black. Compare that with over 90 percent white.

It's worth noting that college baseball scholarships are not the same as your typical athletic scholarship like football. Division-I baseball teams get around a dozen scholarships a year, and can spread them out over many more players than that if they choose. Most college baseball players still have to pay for some or all of their college tuition and expenses.

Because of this, it is often more difficult for a great high school baseball player from an inner city to continue to develop in college than his counterpart from a wealthy, suburban neighborhood. That often means that more white kids get to play college ball than black kids due to financial well being alone.

Is it really Major League Baseball's fault that the number of black players is declining?. . .

How Are the Numbers Devised?

The report went on to give grades for every aspect of MLB employment. Grades were given out based on the following criteria:

Federal affirmative action policies state that the workplace should reflect the percentage of the people in the racial group in the population. Thus, with approximately 24 percent of the population being people of color, an A was achieved if 24 percent of the positions were held by people of color, B if 12 percent of the positions were held by people of color, and C if it had only nine percent. Grades for race below this level were assigned a D for six percent or F for any percent equal to or below five percent.

For issues of gender, an A would be earned if 40 percent of the employees were women, B for 32 percent, C for 27 percent, D for 22 percent and F for anything below that. The 40 percent is also taken from the federal affirmative action standards. The Institute once again acknowledges that even those sports where grades are low generally have better records on race and gender than society as a whole.

Okay, two major problems with doing things this way. One, women don't play baseball, thus are less likely to begin at a ground level and work their way up the corporate ladder. Their lack of experience in the game makes them far less qualified to land jobs that require knowledge of the game, such as scouting. Their inability to have a baseball background limits their ability to rise as effectively or quickly in executive positions. Not that there aren't women qualified to hold many jobs in the game, but I think the game is being unfairly punished or criticized for hiring based on qualifications rather than quotas.

My other major problem with this report is that you can't honestly expect the "workplace" to reflect the population in an instance like this. Of the 40.1% of the "people of color" in baseball, 29 percent of them are Latino, 8 percent black and 2 percent Asian. The problem I have with these numbers is that a large percentage of the Latino players in Major League Baseball don't live in the United States full-time, and many don't speak English well or even remain in the country after their careers are over. These are the people that are most qualified to move on to baseball jobs after playing, but for many reasons of their own, they don't.

Hiring Latinos just to make the numbers right is wrong. Hiring qualified individuals is right. Baseball is a sport and MLB is a league in which you need a baseball background in many positions. You can't just hire people to fill a lot of these jobs.

Why Do Women Need to Be Included in the Numbers?

From the *Associated Press* [2008]:

> Lapchick said 28 percent of employees at baseball's central offices were nonwhite, including 20 percent among senior executives. Women were 42 percent of employees, but 26 percent of the senior executives.
>
> He suggested baseball commissioner Bud Selig pressure clubs more to consider minority candidates. He also said MLB should institute a rule that a woman be considered for all senior job openings, similar to the rule that minority candidates must be interviewed.

I'm going to repeat that last part because it bears repeating. "He also said MLB should institute a rule that a woman be considered for all senior job openings, similar to the rule that minority candidates must be interviewed." Do you really think that making MLB executives interview women and minorities is the right thing to do? I don't mean right as in—make your numbers better—right. I mean right as in—allowing these companies to hire the most qualified individual, man or woman, black or white—and not based only on those "statistics."

I don't want to get into the rights and wrongs of affirmative action, but unfortunately, that's what this report is all about.

The Racial and Gender Report Card

Sixty-one years ago [1947] Jackie Robinson broke Major League Baseball's color barrier in sport and America changed forever as a result. The Racial and Gender Report Card annually asks, "Are we playing fair when it comes to sports? Does everyone, regardless of race or gender, have a chance at bat or to operate a team?". . .

Using data from the 2007 season, The Institute for Diversity and Ethics in Sport conducted an analysis of the racial breakdown of the players, managers and coaches. In addition, the Report Card includes a racial and gender breakdown of the owners, management in the Central Office as well as the team level, top team management, senior administration, professional administration, support staff, physicians, head trainers and broadcasters. . . .

It is imperative that sports teams play the best athletes they have available to win games. The Institute strives to emphasize the business value of diversity to sports organizations when they choose their team on the field and in the office. Diversity initiatives like diversity management training can help change attitudes and increase the applicant pool for open positions. It is obviously the choice of the organization regarding which applicant is the best fit for their ball club, but The Institute wants to illustrate how important it is to have a diverse organization involving individuals who happen to be of a different race or gender because it can provide a different perspective, and possibly a competitive advantage for a win in the board room as well as on the field.

Richard Lapchick, "The 2008 Racial and Gender Report Card: Major League Baseball," April 15, 2008.

I know this will sound sexist, and it probably is, but when a woman plays an inning in the big leagues, then someone can tell a Major League Baseball team that they *have to* interview a woman for their next senior job opening. It's not about male or female, it's about qualifications. If there are qualified females, they will be interviewed and hired when appropriate. Forcing teams to interview a "token" woman is as demeaning to the woman as it is to the team being told how to run their business.

Who Is at Fault for the Numbers?

There is no denying the numbers in this report. There is a reason to question the conclusion they've drawn. There are certainly less black players in the league than there once were. I recall sitting in the visiting dugout before an Arizona Diamondbacks game with Barry Bonds, and Bonds challenging me to name as many black players as I could. Between the two of us, we named maybe 20. That was a few years ago, and it was the first time I ever really realized just how few players eight percent encompassed. I don't know what the solution is to this, or even if there is one. The only thing I took from that conversation was that the game was changing, and no one was really to blame.

Baseball has always changed with the times, and it's always managed to not only keep up, but stay relevant and remain America's Pastime. Getting the numbers where people want them is up to the sport, not the people in it. Baseball is a great game, and it's up to the parents of each generation to introduce their children to it.

If baseball wants to make a difference, it needs to donate more fields and equipment to inner cities. They already do a great job of spreading the game, but if they focus on where they feel they need improvements they could make a big difference.

If racial evenness is what baseball wants, they can do their part to make it happen. But as long as there are so many options for kids to stay entertained, baseball will continue to lose American youths from the game, not just of one race.

> *"A survey by the National Collegiate Athletic Association found colleges have axed 200 men's teams in recent years, with 17,000 slots lost."*

Title IX Is Unfair to Men's Sports

Walter Olson

In the following viewpoint, Walter Olson asserts that compliance to Title IX (the federal law that mandates gender equality in educational programs and activities) unfairly deprives men of the opportunity to participate in sports. Olson further maintains that the enforcers of Title IX completely disregard important determinants—such as a lack of interest in women's athletics among fans and the women themselves—that should be analyzed logically before dropping so many popular men's sports. Walter Olson is a commentator, critic, and author of several books on the American litigation system.

As you read, consider the following questions:

1. Has Title IX affected sports participation in secondary schools, or has it impacted participation only at colleges, according to Walter Olson?

Walter Olson, "Title IX from Outer Space: How Federal Law Is Killing Men's College Sports," WalterOlson.com, October 21, 2006. Reproduced by permission.

2. Why does the author believe that college football should not be included in the quotas for Title IX?

3. Is maintaining an equal proportion of men to women athletes the only way to enforce Title IX?

"Giving Women a Sporting Chance: Cal State Plan Could Be a Template for Nation" jubilated a *Los Angeles Times* editorial. The month was October 1993, and the California State University system had just agreed to settle a National Organization for Women lawsuit by adopting a quota system for varsity sports participation, promising that women's share would come out within 5 percentage points of female enrollment at each of its 19 campuses.

According to the *Times*, this "welcome commitment" would put Cal State in the "vanguard of reform," for which its administration was "to be commended." "Gender fairness in sports is really not that difficult to comprehend," explained the *Times*, with that touch of condescension that so grates on non-feminist ears. "Too many athletic departments just don't"—can you tell where this sentence is headed?—"get it."

Massacre of Men's Sports

The settlement's compliance deadline was set for fall 1998, and by mid-1997 one of its results had become clear: massive cuts in men's sports throughout the Cal State system. In June, Cal State-Northridge dropped its baseball team, which had ranked among the nation's top 20, along with soccer, swimming, and volleyball. Cal State-Bakersfield drastically curtailed its outstanding wrestling program. San Francisco State, Fullerton, Hayward, Chico, Long Beach, and Sonoma all got out of football.

The Cal State-men's-sports massacre made news from coast to coast, and for good reason: As the *Times* headline predicted, it is going to serve as a model for the rest of the country. Last April [2006], the U.S. Supreme Court declined to review a court decision against Brown University, leaving in place an interpretation of the federal Title IX law that has already begun to devastate such men's sports as track, wrestling, swimming, and diving nationwide. A survey by the National Collegiate Athletic Association [NCAA] found colleges have axed 200 men's teams in recent years, with 17,000 slots lost. Gymnastics teams, which numbered 133 as recently as 1975, are down to 32 overall. Even golf, a sport whose popularity in the outside world has soared, is hard hit.

The next targets for Title IX enforcers are elementary and secondary schools. Already, many high schoolers in Florida face a ban on all athletic competition because their schools haven't done well enough at equalizing sports participation. Armed with a 1992 Supreme Court decision which allows complainants to demand cash damages as well as lawyer's fees, litigators and regulators are swarming around the field house.

Lack of Fans and Participants for Women's Sports

The premise of the gender-equity movement is simple: Women's sports should get just as much money, attention, and participation as men's. It's a lovely ambition, acceptable in the end to most college administrators as well as most social reformers. Only two obstacles remain: the fans and the participants.

College football, to begin with, is a huge business, generating fortunes in alumni donations, gate receipts, and broadcast fees. Yet it won't have a real female equivalent as long as women are free to avoid it. (Neither forced watching nor forced playing has yet arisen on the Title IX agenda.) Even aside from male-female differences in strength and stature, extremes of physical competition and the buzz of danger just don't play the same role in women's lives as in men's either as players or as spectators. As *National Review*'s Kate O'Beirne has pointed out, men made up a substantial majority of the television audience for the women's NCAA basketball finals.

In questionnaires of prospective Brown students, 50 percent of the men but only 30 percent of the women expressed interest in trying out for athletics. Intramural sports were open to all at Brown, but eight times as many men took part as women. Nor is it easy to argue that the dead hand of bygone male supremacy is the problem. Women at Vassar participate in varsity sports at a rate 13 percent lower than do men, even though Vassar was a women's college until 1969.

"Including football in counting the numbers is unreasonable," Olympic high jumper Amy Acuff told one reporter. "At my school [UCLA], they cut men's swimming and gymnastics so they could start water polo and soccer for women. It broke my heart because those men's teams were really good, and a lot of the women they brought into the new sports weren't serious athletes." (The defunct UCLA diving and swimming program had garnered 16 Olympic gold medals and 41 individual national titles.)

All About Questions—Not Common Sense

Tough, say the hard-liners at the U.S. Department of Education's Office of Civil Rights [OCR], which "has exhibited an astonishing indifference to the destruction of athletic opportunities for males," according to University of Chicago wrestling coach Leo Kocher. Anyone at all can file a complaint that triggers an OCR investigation, and such probes, as *Pittsburgh Post-Gazette* sportswriter Lori Shontz observes, are not always known for their sophistication and subtlety. Staffers who swooped down on Johns Hopkins University, for instance, demanded to know why the women's basketballs were smaller than the men's, not realizing that "women's basketballs are smaller by design to accommodate smaller hands."

As usual in Washington, the quota-enforcers heatedly deny that quotas are actually mandatory, insisting that schools can comply by passing one of two other tests. They can show that women are satisfied with existing offerings—but then a complaint itself is apt to serve as evidence of dissatisfaction. Or schools can show a pattern of continued expansion of women's programs, which is to say continued progress toward proportionality. In practice, according to the American Football Coaches Association and other critics, proportionality is the "primary emphasis of enforcement," and the other two tests, though they may furnish the regulators some facade of deniability against quota charges, offer no enduring safe harbor of compliance.

In the Brown case, the federal court rebuffed the university's effort to offer evidence that men were more interested in athletics. Are women's teams undersubscribed and men's oversubscribed? Then a university must have fallen short in finding ways to make the women's programs attractive. Is it easier for women at a given level of achievement or commitment to obtain athletic scholarships than it is for men? Too bad: The university may lose anyway, unless it's brought the overall head count into line.

Nor can educators necessarily get off the hook by pointing to other demographic or behavioral variables. The student body at Cal State-Bakersfield, reports Elizabeth Arens in *Policy Review*, is 64 percent female and includes many women in their 40s and 50s who are upgrading their education after launching families and disinclined to pursue varsity sports.

Feminists' Exploitation of Title IX

"The women's advocacy groups strongly oppose any effort to survey interest in athletics because they do not like the results," charges Chuck Neinas, executive director of the College Football Association, who says the current state of legal interpretation "will make it difficult, if not impossible, for those universities that sponsor football to comply with Title IX."

Understanding Title IX

Under Title IX, there must be proportionality between men's and women's teams based on the total enrollment at the school. If a university has 16,000 students and an overall enrollment of 60 percent females, then under Title IX, there should be more women's teams than men's teams to create equality. This proportionality can be satisfied by a school in three different ways.

First, the amount of participation should be proportional between men and women.

Secondly, the law requires that female and male student-athletes receive athletic scholarship funding and spending proportional to their participation and this means having equal facilities, equipment and opportunities afforded to the players.

The third part of the law states the school must show a continuous history of expanding opportunities for the underrepresented gender.

Alyssa Benedetto, "College Athletes Affected by Title IX,"
The Review, *November 20, 2007.*

Feminist litigators make little secret of their animus toward football, many evidently agreeing with University of Wisconsin-Milwaukee professor Margaret Carlisle Duncan that it's "an institution that promotes male dominance." Where it can't be axed entirely, they favor at least reducing the number of players on rosters, as Cal State-Fresno and other institutions have reluctantly done. College teams play with larger rosters than the pros, partly because they can't rely on midseason signups or trades to replace sidelined regular players.

Ironically, colleges with standout football teams, being flush with revenues for scholarships and equipment, have the easiest time expanding women's sports. Although top-division football as a whole makes money, it is made unevenly, with some strong teams raking in the receipts and others running deficits. Title IX activists urge colleges to boot money-losing pigskin teams, though it seems unlikely that a conference whose cellar-dwellers dropped out could for long achieve a Lake Wobegon effect and consist entirely of teams with favorable win-lose records.

In any event, the head count, not money, is what's often really at legal issue. Wrestling is among the least expensive sports to sustain. Princeton refused to accept a $2.3 million alumni gift intended as an endowment to save its 90-year-old men's wrestling team, just as the University of Southern California did when alumni tried to save its men's swimming program. Roster cutbacks for "big" men's sports, a common feminist proposal, aid compliance efforts not so much because they save pots of money—the non-star "walk-ons" dropped are typically already playing without scholarships, travel, or equipment subsidies—but because they keep down the number of male bodies.

Meddlesome Equal Opportunity Commission

Of course, the Equal Employment Opportunity Commission can't resist making things worse. Last October [2005], it put out new guidelines arm-twisting colleges to pay coaches of women's teams as much as they do men's. The guidelines do start with a token concession that not every volleyball coach may be entitled to the salary of a Big Ten football wizard, but from then on it's mostly bad news. Comparisons between dissimilar sports? No problem. Offers based on market rates or current pay levels will be suspect: "Cultural and social factors may have artificially inflated men's coaches' salaries."

The guidelines hint that if colleges can't show that they've advertised and promoted men's and women's squads equally, women's coaches should win salary-dispute cases. Of course, to hype a fanless team may be to throw good money after bad: In one well-known case, the USC [University of Southern California] men's basketball program brought in 90 times as much revenue as the women's. The agency also suggests a college may lose a case if it "sets up weekly media interviews" for a red-hot men's team but not its languishing female equivalent.

In the whole Title IX controversy, incidentally, it appears next to impossible to find anyone willing to criticize the law in principle. Sure, enforcement has gone haywire and the results are crazy, but everyone hastens to add that of course they just adore the law itself.

As for the old idea that universities in a free society should be entitled to make their own decisions—well, that notion, like so many men's track teams, is on its last lap.

"Those concerned with the modest shrinking of men's sports should think more carefully about wasted resources and less about taking resources away from female athletes."

Title IX Is Not Unfair to Men's Sports

Andrew Zimbalist

In the following viewpoint, Andrew Zimbalist defends Title IX's efforts to achieve gender equity in athletic opportunities and, in fact, he asserts that Title IX needs to reach even further to achieve its goal. Zimbalist maintains that athletic opportunities for men have not been significantly reduced. But for those Title IX detractors who claim otherwise, he suggests alternative methods of achieving Title IX compliance, including reducing the number of team coaches as well as lowering their salaries. Sports Economist Andrew Zimbalist is the author of several books, including In the Best Interests of Baseball? The Revolutionary Reign of Bud Selig.

Andrew Zimbalist, *The Bottom Line: Observations and Arguments on the Sports Business.* Philadelphia, PA: Temple University Press, 2006. Copyright © 2006 by Andrew Zimbalist. All rights reserved. Reproduced by permission.

As you read, consider the following questions:

1. According to Andrew Zimbalist, do most college athletic programs earn a monetary surplus?

2. How does the salary of a football coach at a large university compare with that of a coach for a professional football franchise, according to the author?

3. In past years has the National Collegiate Athletic Association supported Title IX, according to Andrew Zimbalist?

After an initial burst of progress following its passage in 1972, Title IX did little to promote gender equity in intercollegiate athletics during the 1980s. The Civil Rights Restoration Act of 1987 and subsequent court cases, however, reinvigorated the advance during the 1990s. The share of women among all intercollegiate athletes increased from 33.4 percent in 1990–91 to 39.9 percent in 1997–98.

While this growth marks substantial improvement, it is clear that women still have a long road to travel before gender equity is attained. In Division I during 1997–98, women accounted for 41 percent of all athletic-scholarship money, 40 percent of all athletes, 33 percent of all sports-operating expenditures, 30 percent of recruitment spending, and 27 percent of base salaries for head coaches. Beyond this, female athletes still play in inferior facilities, stay in lower-category hotels on the road, eat in cheaper restaurants, benefit from smaller promotional budgets, have fewer assistant coaches, and so on. Cedric Dempsey, the NCAA's [National Collegiate Athletic Association's] executive director, assessed the status of gender equity in college sports in October 1999 as follows: "Improvements are being made, but being made much too slowly. . . . We must continue to add programs for women and dedicate more resources to women's programs on our campuses at a faster rate."

Yet the progress toward gender equity is too rapid for some. The Center for Individual Rights, the Independent Women's Forum, and members of the collegiate wrestling community are pressing the presidential candidates, the courts, and other constituencies to reinterpret Title IX or change the law. They argue that it is wrong for the number of participants in some men's sports to be capped or for other men's sports to be eliminated in the furtherance of meeting quantitative Title IX standards.

The Problem Is Money

While it is easy to sympathize with those who would prefer to see more opportunities for male athletes, it is unrealistic to think that growing women's sports alone will be sufficient to achieve gender equity in the near or intermediate future. The problem, of course, is money. Of the 973 colleges in the NCAA, only a dozen or so have athletic programs that run a true surplus in any given year. The accounting imbroglios of college sports finances are too pervasive to permit an elucidation of this claim here. Suffice it to say that the University of Michigan, which perennially ranks in the top twenty in both football and basketball, has a football stadium with a capacity of 111,000 that has sold out every game since the mid-1980s, and earns more than $5 million annually in licensing revenues, ran a reported $2.5 million deficit in athletics last year. Thus, unless universities and state governments are willing to subsidize further intercollegiate athletic programs at the expense of other educational activities, there must be some redistribution of resources within athletics.

The Title IX critics claim that men are being shafted. While it is true that some men's teams have had the number of players capped, and a few sports at some schools have been cut, the larger picture does not suggest significant net losses for male athletes. Hardest hit has been men's wrestling, where the number of colleges sponsoring teams has fallen from 264 in

1993–94 to 246 in 1997–98, a modest 6.8 percent decline. Some schools have limited the number of walk-ons in football and other men's sports, but the average Division I football team still has 103 players.

Overall, between 1978 and 1996 the total number of men's sports teams in all three NCAA divisions increased by seventy-four. After falling 12 percent between 1985 and 1996, the number of male athletes grew 6 percent during the past three years. In 1997–98, 203,686 male and 135,110 female athletes were playing college sports.

The Title IX detractors argue that it is both understandable and acceptable for men's sports to receive differential resources because it is men's basketball and football that produce the net revenues to fund the other sports. First, this argument ignores the fact that men's wrestling, swimming, squash, tennis, track and field, etc., all are net revenue losers, and if a market criterion is applied, any one of them may be subject to reduction or elimination. Second, both Title IX and the courts' interpretation of it make clear that market forces do not alter the goal of gender equity. Indeed, college sports programs happily enjoy numerous tax benefits as well as the privilege of not paying their athletes a salary on the grounds that they are sponsoring amateur activities. Prevailing college ethos requires that academic resources be equally available to men and women. It is duplicitous for universities to accept the fruits of amateurism for men's sports and then invoke business principles when it comes to funding for women's sports. Third, although the absolute measures of women's participation and scholarship support are higher at Division IA schools, the relative measures are lower than they are at Division IAAA (programs without football) and Division II schools.

Other Options for Resources Are Available

More important, there are more attractive options available than reducing or eliminating men's sports. Currently, men's programs are extravagantly funded. Men's coaches on the leading basketball and football teams receive compensation packages routinely between $700,000 and $1.4 million (although their base salaries, to which women's coaches' salaries are compared, will normally be in the $125,000–$200,000 range). The coaches are getting paid with the money saved by not paying the players they (or their assistants) recruit. It is well beyond the salary that a competitive market would offer them. What free market would pay strikingly similar total salaries to the coaches on the top three dozen football and basketball teams when the average revenue generated by a Division IA football team is 2.7 times that of a Division IA basketball team? And what market would pay a Division IA football coach roughly the same total salary as an NFL [National Football League] team coach, when an average NFL generates ten times the revenue of an average Division IA football team?

So one obvious place to find resources to promote gender equity without diminishing men's sports is the coaches' salaries. Would it be too radical to require that a head coach's compensation package not exceed that of the university president? Such a reform would save dozens of schools in the neighborhood of $1 million—enough to finance two Division I swimming and diving teams or one ice-hockey team.

Another place to find resources is in the excess number of coaches in certain sports. The average Division IA football team carries 10.3 assistant coaches, at an average salary of more than $60,000, plus benefits and perquisites. Cutting the number here by three would save enough to support a college tennis team.

The scholarship limit for men's football is eighty-five. There are eleven players on the field at a time. Even with three separate platoons with different players for offense, defense, and special teams and a punter and place kicker, a team needs only thirty-five players. NFL teams have forty-five–man rosters with a taxi squad of seven players. Why do Division IA teams need eighty-five scholarship players? College coaches will maintain that they need more players than the NFL because of injuries. When an NFL player is hurt, the team adds a player. College football does not have the same flexibility, the coaches say. But what about the fact that most Division IA teams carry twenty to fifty walk-ons (nonscholarship players), bringing the total rosters to well over one hundred? There is no compelling reason why the number of scholarships could not be reduced to sixty, saving each school $350,000 or more— approximately the budget of a Division I wrestling team.

Finally, a long shot—but one worth pursuing—is that MLB [Major League Baseball] teams spend nearly $10 million each on their minor-league and player-development systems. NFL and NBA [National Basketball Association] teams don't have minor leagues; universities do it for them. The NCAA also cooperates with the leagues in player draft and eligibility regulations. Is there any reason why the NFL and NBA should not be contributing to the player-development programs at U.S. colleges?

Title IX Is Worth Fighting For

It is heartening that Cedric Dempsey issues public declarations that the progress of Title IX is too slow. When the NCAA feels strongly about a matter, it has devoted resources to ensure its development. During 1972–74, for instance, the NCAA spent $300,000 lobbying against the full implementation of Title IX. In 1976, it invested additional funds in challenging Title IX in the courts. One hopes that this time around, the NCAA will convert its words into actions on behalf of Title IX.

Kimberly Schuld, manager for special projects at the Independent Women's Forum, asserts that the implementation of Title IX has created a quota system and that colleges are starting "women's programs like bowling, squash and tiddlywinks to say they have more women's programs and are in compliance." Schuld's sarcasm to the contrary, women have showed that they are interested in participating in intercollegiate sports when the opportunities are there. Currently, more than 2.25 million girls are playing interscholastic sports in high school— more than enough to supply enthusiastic players for larger numbers of women's college teams. Attendance at women's sporting contests is growing every year, as are television ratings. Until women's college sports are supported at levels similar to those of the men for close to a generation in time, it will be impossible to assess their long-run potential. In the meantime, those concerned with the modest shrinking of men's sports should think more carefully about wasted resources and less about taking resources away from female athletes.

"Overall, the kids playing club sports are from middle, upper-middle and wealthy families. Poor and working-class kids are by and large left out."

Only the Wealthy Can Afford Competitive Sports

Regan McMahon

Regan McMahon, deputy book editor at the San Francisco Chronicle *and author of numerous articles, music reviews, and book reviews, explains in the following viewpoint the rise in popularity of elite sports clubs and how costly it is to be a member of such clubs. McMahon cites the opinions of several experts to illustrate the manner in which elite sports clubs exploit youth for financial gain and detrimentally impact disadvantaged youth.*

As you read, consider the following questions:

1. According to athletic trainer Carlos Arreaga, what message is being sent by elite sports club organizations?

2. Does Arreaga believe that kids with genetically gifted athletic abilities need to play on club sports teams to become successful athletes?

3. According to Regan McMahon, what is one of the biggest cultural shifts among high school athletes that resulted from the rise in club sports?

The second biggest change in the evolution of youth sports, after the increased opportunity for and participation of girls, is the rise of the elite clubs. Up until the early 1990s, the pinnacle of many young people's sports experience was playing for their high school team. Some athletes pursuing individual sports like ice skating or gymnastics might have had the Olympics as their goal from an early age, and may have moved to be with a special coach and worked with additional personal trainers. But the vast majority of kids played team sports in city recreational and parochial leagues or at the YMCA, Boys and Girls Clubs or the Police Activities League when they were in grade school and middle school. If they were particularly talented and motivated, they made their high school teams, and at that point ramped up their skill level as well as their time commitment to practice and training.

It was the high school stars who caught the eye of college recruiters. Some got scholarships; some made the college team but paid their own way. Some played only intramural collegiate sports and cherished memories of being on their high school team—the tradition, the local rivalries, following in the cleat and sneaker steps of community and possibly family members who had gone before them.

That was then.

Now private clubs offer the highest level, most competitive play. For a membership fee, between $500 and $5,500 a year, parents buy what they believe is the best opportunity for their child to get top-notch coaching and—if the child sticks with it through high school—get seen by college recruiters at the many weekend and holiday tournaments that are the clubs' lifeblood. For many parents, the long-term goal is that coveted college scholarship. Even when they're signing up a kid as young as 6.

And it's not just soccer, though the soccer club system came first. Now there are clubs for most other sports, many of which are part of the Amateur Athletic Union [AAU]. There's AAU basketball, football, baseball, swimming, gymnastics, hockey and lacrosse. And what comes along with making the cut is a big jump in time commitment—two to three practices a week, in addition to two games per regular weekend and up to five or six games in a tournament—and cost: for dues, uniform and tournament fees, as well for the extensive traveling and overnight accommodations in what becomes virtually a year-round sport. The AAU reports that participation among girls nationally has gone up 55 percent in a decade, with 129,000 girls on AAU teams in 2005.

On top of club fees, many parents of club players are paying for personal trainers, commonly for kids 12 and up and occasionally for kids as young as 8. In my area, a pitching coach is $65 an hour, a goalie coach $100 an hour. Besides individual trainers, families can now turn to athletic training facilities, which are springing up around the country. Velocity Sports Performance, a national chain of state-of-the-art sports training centers based in Alpharetta, Georgia, has sites in 100 cities in the United States, including St. Louis, Kansas City, Philadelphia, Los Angeles, Alexandria, Virginia, and three in the Bay Area, in San Carlos, Concord and Dublin, in the heart of suburban club play. Founded in 1999, Velocity brings the latest sports training techniques from university and professional athletic programs to improve and maximize the athletic ability of athletes of all ages and skill levels. At Velocity you can "train like a pro," as its promotional materials say, even if you're an 8-year-old Little Leaguer. The price for kids 8 to 11 for three one-hour sessions a week for a month: $465. (The price goes down for three-, six- and 12-month packages.)

There are also sports summer camps to augment a player's training and conditioning in what might be called the off-season, except that the kids are still going to practices and playing their sport, even if they're not playing games for a seasonal record. Often there is an intimidation factor at play when players are informed of an "optional" camp or practice. . . .

"The message is being sent out there by these club organizations that your kids will be left behind if they don't participate at this level," says Carlos Arreaga, staff athletic trainer at Bishop O'Dowd High School, in Oakland, California. "And one of the things that's driving that is they're making money off of it. As much as they say they're doing this for the kids, is that truly what the philosophy of the clubs are? It's ultimately based on competition and who has the better club. I feel like there are some hypocritical messages being sent.

"It's really kind of sad because I think our kids, to some degree, are being used for financial gain and ultimately for adults. This is a trickle-down effect from professional to college sports. Years ago the talk was about college athletes and how they're being exploited for the universities' benefit. Now youth are being exploited to some degree for the adults' benefit. And that's not a healthy thing.

"In addition to working here at the high school as an athletic trainer, I've also worked as a personal trainer, and I'm also a strength and conditioning specialist and I'm certified to work with high school athletes doing personal training. I've done that for a few years and I've really thought a lot about this, and I've been very much in conflict about what's going on with youth sports. And I'm really pondering: Hey, is this really the right thing to be doing by running summer camps with kids and doing the training? Where is the balance? And what's the right thing to do? Because I don't want to contribute to that. So maybe I am, and I do feel conflicted about it."

But is it possible to make a high school team these days if you haven't played club?

"The kids who are really talented could," says Arreaga. "It's the borderline kids where it would really make a difference.

Even at the college level, those kids who are skilled are probably going to make it regardless. For whatever reason they're genetically gifted, and those types of kids are going to be fine down the road. It's the kids who are average to below average who might need to put in extra time. But the perception among the kids is they have to play club or they won't make it."

"I think it's one of those myths parents buy into that if you don't keep up with the Joneses, you're not going to make the high school team," says Bob Tewksbury, former Cy Young Award–winning pitcher for the St. Louis Cardinals, who also pitched for the Minnesota Twins. Tewksbury is now a sports psychologist for the Boston Red Sox and host of a radio show in New Hampshire called *Sports from a Different Perspective*, as well as a youth sports coach and father of a son, 14, and a daughter, 12, both of whom play sports.

The significance of innate talent, Tewksbury says, is often overlooked by parents who believe they can produce a star athlete by following all the right training steps. He agrees with the American Academy of Pediatrics, which issued a policy statement in 2000 recommending that children not specialize in a sport until adolescence, when they are emotionally and physically more mature. The academy suggests holding off from specializing until age 12 or 13. Tewksbury would wait even a few years longer.

"In my experience as having played at the highest level of the pros for a long time, there's a thing called talent that I think people underestimate. And I think when parents elect to put children in early participation programs, for example at age 10, committing to being a full-time, year-round soccer player, they think that's going to equate to talent. Will their skill improve? Yes, it will. But you don't really know what your talent level is until you mature.

"The problem is the professionalization of youth sports. There are early-blooming kids and early-developing kids who are always going to have greater success because of their physical structure, and the later-maturing kids were traditionally held back because they weren't as good. Now we're labeling kids as good or not good at the age of 12, which is crazy! The research says specialization should start around age 15 or so. So if you have talent with the maturation process, now we can see how good you are. It's not determined when you're 10."

Tewksbury also objects to club coaches who would discourage or prevent kids from playing on their high school team. "And for what reason? For that 1 in 100 who gets that scholarship to play maybe on a Division I team? The odds of playing at a Division I level or getting a scholarship to play are incredibly against you. So the trade-off is what?

"I think it's a myth. It's a tidal wave of a belief system that's wrong. The elite club teams cultivate that. They say if you don't play for me, then you're not going to be able to play for that team. And parents believe that."

The devaluing of high school team participation is one of the biggest cultural shifts that have occurred thanks to the rise to club sports. Many club coaches discourage or prevent their players from going out for the high school team, even though the schools and the leagues in many cases guarantee there won't be a scheduling conflict. In my state, for example, the California Interscholastic League mandates that club soccer cannot run concurrently with the school soccer season. "The good news is the seasons don't conflict," one soccer mom of a club player told me. "The bad news is soccer lasts the whole damn year."

Yet even without conflicting seasons, some club athletes are still pressured not to play for their high school because they might get injured and become unavailable to play for the club team. Others simply believe that the level of play is not as competitive and that college recruiters will focus on the club teams, so why should they bother playing for the high school? What's in it for me? Fading is the value of representing something outside yourself, bigger than yourself: your community, your school. The high school club player is often driving toward a more personal goal: being seen by the recruiter, getting a scholarship.

Mike Riera is a nationally known parenting expert, the family and adolescent counselor for the *CBS Saturday Early Show* and a frequent guest on *Oprah* and NPR [National Public Radio], author of *Staying Connected to Your Teenager* and co-author with Joe Di Prisco of *Field Guide to the American Teenager*, and head of the K-8 Redwood Day School, in Oakland, California. Riera, a multi-sport star athlete in high school who was captain of his basketball team at Wesleyan University, thinks it's a shame that kids are being discouraged from playing for their high schools. He told me, "You know, as corny as pep rallies are, it's a powerful experience in a kid's life when you're out there as a member of the team and introduced in front of the student body and everyone cheers for you and it's homecoming and everyone knows that's going on, versus on a club team, where it's just the parents and the players.

"My dad was a Hall of Fame high school basketball coach. And he was the P.E. teacher at the school. He saw the kids all day. And he would know when Johnny or Sherry's got a problem, because it would show up in practice, he would see them at school, he could call them into his office. He could really affect their lives. Whereas a club coach just sees them at practice. You don't *see* the rest of their life. I think club coaches miss the chance to really impact a kid's life by not being at school all the time." . . .

The level of opportunity varies from sport to sport. In soccer and volleyball, for example, club players have a clear advantage over non-club athletes as far as making the high school team is concerned, and in being seen by college recruiters. Travel-team baseball—called Extreme Baseball—is a relatively new phenomenon, having geared up mainly in the

The Expense of Competitive Sports

Do you have a list like this one?

　　Football: $175

　　Refundable equipment fee: $35

　　Cleats: $80

　　Required fundraising event: $35

　　More required fundraising: $40

　　End of season party: $15

　　Gift for coach: $10

And that doesn't even include the gas to run them back and forth, the time spent doing your required volunteer hours or the friends you've alienated trying to sell them candy bars or coupon books! If it seems like our children's activities are getting more and more expensive and time consuming with every passing year—it's because they are. Many families have found that sports have become a luxury they can't afford.

Teri Brown, "Pay to Play:
The Expense of Extracurricular Activities," iParenting.com.

new millennium, so it's difficult to gauge its impact on athletic careers. (But it's having a big impact on the family: wiping out summer vacation plans.) High school basketball and football programs still seem open to raw talent the coaches can develop. That's how it used to be: Kids went to tryouts as freshmen and the most talented athletes or kids who showed the most promise got picked. Today the playing field is less level.

In fact, the rise of the elite clubs is changing the complexion of youth teams and the socioeconomic realities of high school athletics. Club teams are expensive, with the high cost of uniforms, fees and travel. A few kids may get scholarships or financial aid—and not all club teams offer these—but overall, the kids playing club sports are from middle, upper-middle and wealthy families. Poor and working-class kids are by and large left out, unless they get discovered playing street ball or playing in a recreation league and get sponsored to join a club.

Former Manchester United soccer player Gordon Hill, commenting on the state of American youth soccer in Jamie Trecker's column on the FOX Soccer Channel Web site, said, "I think we're missing 20 to 25 percent of possible kids in the pool—conservatively that's 2 to 3 million kids who don't play because their parents cannot afford it."

A soccer dad posted this response to Trecker's column on the issue of U.S. soccer becoming a sport of the well-off: "In the pay to play system, the buyers (parents/players) have three resources: talent, money and time. The sellers (clubs) have one resource—the game; with a hierarchy of quality. The higher the quality, the more buyers' resources they will attract. A club can sustain itself on volume (3,000 rec players at $50 a head), or it can make it on margin (300 elite players at $500 a head). They just have to compute the costs of goods sold and set the prices."

If high school and college teams give preference to club players, then ipso facto they're favoring the privileged over the disadvantaged, widening the gap between rich and poor in an arena that used to serve as a great equalizer.

Joe Freeman, a writer for *The Oregonian* newspaper, summed up the situation succinctly in an October 2005 article: "Proponents say club sports improve the quality of high school play, offering rare opportunities to elite athletes and providing a year-round outlet for teenagers who wish to focus on a specific sport. But others say club sports—which can cost thousands of dollars a season—cater to the wealthy, decrease the number of high school athletes who play multiple sports and increase the demands on athletes when sports are meant to be fun."

We have to ask ourselves, is this the best thing for our kids? For our schools? For our families? And what is that year-round high-level play doing to all those young bodies?

Periodical Bibliography

The following articles have been selected to supplement the diverse views presented in this chapter.

Joshua Charles	"Defeating Racism with Sports," *The Voice*, February 12, 2007.
Murray Chass	"Dodgers Are Allowed to Bypass Rule on Minority Hiring," *International Herald Tribune*, November 1, 2007.
Frank Deford	"Unfair Advantage: As Title IX Turns 35, the Law Needs to Be Re-Evaluated," *Sports Illustrated*, June 22, 2007.
Lisa Fabrizio	"Racism and Sports," RenewAmerica.us, February 23, 2006.
Sara Hoffman Jurand	"Equality in Sports Is Still Elusive Goal for Girl Athletes," *Trial*, September 1, 2004.
Anne Kadet	"Parents Spare No Expense in Children's Sports," *Smart Money*, June 27, 2008.
Richard Lapchick	"MLB's Diversity Would Have Jackie Shaking His Head," ESPN.com, April 15, 2008.
William C. Rhoden	"Addressing Racism's Constant Hum in U.S. Sports," *International Herald Tribune*, May 25, 2008.
Alex Rubin	"Inequality Driven from Equality," *The Spectrum*, May 19, 2008.
Leonard Shapiro and Mark Maske	"NFL Improves in Minority Hiring," *Washington Post*, January 29, 2005.

OPPOSING
VIEWPOINTS®
SERIES

CHAPTER 4

Is Drug Use a Problem in Sports?

Chapter Preface

Steroids and other banned substances used for the purpose of boosting athletic performance have been getting a lot of negative attention in the past several years. American cyclist Floyd Landis was stripped of his 2006 Tour De France cycling medal after testing positive for a banned substance. Marion Jones not only relinquished her Olympic medals but also was sentenced to six months in jail for lying under oath about her use of performance-enhancing drugs. And the Mitchell Report, released in December 2007, detailed the use of steroids and human growth hormones (HGH) by approximately eighty-nine major league baseball players. Though some people would argue that steroids should be legalized, presently they are legal only with a prescription. In general, concerns have focused on anabolic steroids, HGH, and other banned drugs, such as erythropoietin, or EPO, which boosts blood oxygen content. Gene doping, however, is the newest threat and involves injecting genes or genetic material into the body to make it stronger, faster, or more resilient.

Given the risks to their reputations and health, why do athletes continue to use these performance-enhancing drugs? One answer could be that they are willing to do everything possible to perfect their performance, to do whatever it takes to be the best. In other words: success at all costs. And that message is trickling down to pervade the mindset of the nation's youth.

Participation in sports plays a major role in the development of most American children. Approximately 45 million kids, ages six through eighteen, participate in either a school or community-based athletic program. And these young athletes can be especially vulnerable to taking performance-enhancing drugs because they haven't yet established emotional or physical maturity and a firm sense of self. Often, the self-esteem of these young people relies wholly on other people's admiration of their athletic success. In his article, "Professional and Youth Sports: A Story of Drugs and Values," motivational speaker and self-esteem expert Robert Brooks wrote, "A need for approval is a powerful motivator to do whatever it takes to be accepted and loved by one's parents or other significant adults." Learning by example from sports stars, some youth—desiring to gain a competitive edge—readily accept the credo that cheating is okay if you can get away with it.

However, young athletes can glean positive lessons from the recent furor over steroids, including what it means to create and follow ethical value systems, how to win and lose with dignity, and how to earn respect through perseverance and unwavering resolve. Brooks continued in his article, "We must teach our children that shortcuts to success rarely, if ever, lead to the desired results." Mari Holden, the 2000 world champion and Olympic silver medalist in the sport of cycling, agrees. In her testimony before the U.S. Congress Government Reform committee, Holden said, "Far too little has been heard from the athletes who strive to participate in sport using the right substances; namely, personal accountability, commitment, hard work, and integrity."

The subject of steroid use has become quite controversial and is passionately debated among experts and athletes alike. The authors in the following chapter discuss this and other issues concerning the use of drugs in sports.

> *"It is very concerning when high school coaches, parents and administrators reflect denial about a drug situation that national health statistics reveal as alarming."*

Performance-Enhancing Drugs Should Be Banned from Sports

Steve Courson

Steve Courson, former Tampa Bay Buccaneers professional football player and admitted former steroid user who died in November 2005, describes in the following viewpoint many of the risks associated with steroid use. He maintains that steroids are particularly dangerous for young people because they are not yet physically developed, and also because steroid use encourages the misguided "win at all costs" mentality. Courson offers possible solutions, such as educating school nurses, to eradicate the use of performance-enhancing drugs among adolescents.

As you read, consider the following questions:

1. According to Steve Courson, when was the first known emergence of anabolic steroids?

Steve Courson, "Performance-Enhancement and the Future," statement to Committee on Government Reform, House of Representatives, April 25, 2005. Reproduced by permission.

2. Does the National Football League (NFL) randomly test players for steroid use?

3. According to Courson, who besides youth are receiving a "win at all costs" message from elite sports?

Esteemed members of Congress, representatives of the press, citizens and NFL [National Football League] personnel. We are all here discussing a very unpleasant reality of modern sport. I come to you experiencing a unique perspective in this dilemma. I was a member of arguably one of the greatest teams in NFL history, a lineman, a strength athlete, Super Bowl Champion, admitted former steroid user, former high school coach and finally one who has given hundreds of prevention education programs in schools dealing with performance-enhancing drugs. I have been literally in the trenches as a user and as an educator who has observed the teenage situation first hand. The predicament with these various substances is not just an issue with the NFL but all sports and society as a whole. I believe more than anything it is reflective of the negative realities of modern training combined with the current intensity of competition.

This dilemma has spread to our high schools and junior high schools. It was essentially spawned out of a combination of competitive zeal, advancing science and societal ignorance. I commend President [George W.] Bush with bringing this issue to the attention of the American people with his comments in his 2004 State of the Union Address. Pressure to win should not be a foreign emotion to any politician here, for you have faced the intensity of elections.

Risks Associated with Steroid Use

Experiencing the emotional trauma of a life threatening disease, dilated cardiomyopathy is a humbling experience. This fact was greatly amplified when previously I was an elite athlete. My illness and miraculous recovery have led me to contemplate these issues deeper than most. When I first started seeing heart symptoms in 1985 and was suspicious of their potential relationship with anabolic steroids, perhaps the scariest part was recognizing how little the medical community knew about these drugs. Today we still don't know whether my illness or the late Raider [Oakland, California football team] great Lyle Alzado's T-Cell lymphoma was related to the use of anabolic hormones because of the lack of definitive long-term longitudinal research. I do believe that higher body weights assisted by the use of drugs do create greater vital organ risk factors. Personally, the recovery effects the drugs had on my enhanced ability to train were the most addicting aspect of their use. The lack of research becomes increasingly more precarious for society in general as human growth hormone (HGH) and testosterone now are being promoted as the new "fountain of youth" in hormone replacement anti-aging therapy in clinics nationwide.

The short-term male hormone side effects of these drugs are well documented as well as the greater risks associated with adolescent use. Performance-enhancing drug use is as inappropriate for teenagers as any recreational drug abuse. Current estimates range from [frac12] to one million adolescent users, one study estimated close to 80,000 eighth graders. The irony of young people using these drugs is that their bodies are geared for growth naturally without them. Using improperly at a young age training-wise is as potentially negative to physical development as introducing extremely heavy weight training to a bone structure still growing. This can only be counterproductive.

A Brief History

Anabolic steroids systemically had their first known historical emergence with the world dominant Soviet Olympic Weightlifting teams of the 1950's. As the story goes the Soviet team physician and the United States team physician Dr. John Zie-

© John S. Pritchett.

gler were having dinner and drinks after the world weightlifting championships in Vienna in 1954. Apparently the Soviet team doctor got tipsy and spilled the beans that the Soviets were using testosterone in their weight lifters. This prompted Ziegler to work with the Ciba pharmaceutical company and our weight lifters, many who trained in York, PA. He helped create the oral anabolic steroid Dianabol, in 1958. Pandora's Box was now opened and by 1963 the drugs had spread to professional football. The San Diego Chargers hired the first strength coach in professional football, Alvin Roy. Mr. Roy had worked with the U.S. Olympic Weight Lifting team and understood the effectiveness of Dianabol. He later worked with the [Kansas City] Chiefs, [Dallas] Cowboys and [Oakland] Raiders while passing in 1979.

Essentially this type of drug use was not viewed as cheating. By the 1970's, it is safe to say that the "diffusion of innovation" with anabolic steroids had spread to a certain degree to every NFL team. However, strength athletes across the sports spectrum were soon to realize the effectiveness of various anabolic hormones combined with proper diet and training. Pressure to win, medical ignorance and man's never ending search to enhance training played a crucial role. The NFL, at this time under commissioner Pete Rozelle had no enforced policy so NFL players and coaches became victims of the times. By the 1980's the use of anabolic hormones was widespread and the NFL responded by starting announced testing in 1987. Steroid use officially became cheating in the NFL in 1989 when punitive testing began with fines and suspensions imposed with those who violated the league's substance abuse policy. In 1989, NFL players such as Bill Fralic approached commissioner Tagliabue wanting random testing to be instituted to hopefully level the playing field. Commissioner Tagliabue responded favorably by initiating a random testing program tougher than any other professional team sport in the United States. However, is it enough?

The BALCO Investigations [Bay Area Laboratory Co-Operative, the supplement company that supplied steroids to athletes] has been informative in evaporating some of the existing myth's surrounding drug use in elite sport. It is often been stated that only "a few bad apples" are using performance-enhancing substances. Yet, the allegations in BALCO involve some of the world's best athletes from across the sports spectrum. The significance of the threat that "designer steroids" present to modern testing technology has also been a product of the scandal. New evidence reported by a CBS *60 Minutes* telecast involving the Carolina Panthers also reflect testing loopholes. Human growth hormone (HGH) and testosterone in low doses have long been a strategy used by athletes in many sports to avoid detection. In training for power, strength and size it is common knowledge that HGH works better when used with an androgen and testosterone is most definitely an androgen. . . .

Adolescent Use

It is very concerning when high school coaches, parents and administrators reflect denial about a drug situation that national health statistics reveal as alarming. What kind of leaders are they? Unfortunately we as a society base the hiring and firing of coaches even in high school on primarily winning and losing. This reflects the "win at all costs" mentality of elite sport. This may be appropriate when big money is at stake, but is it elsewhere? This mentality in youth sport needs to change. How can coaches teach valuable lessons about preparing youth for life when their value is based only on wins and losses? It is not just our youth that are receiving mixed messages from big time sport, but our coaches and parents as well. We as a society in this age can ill-afford these misguided philosophical messages of winning regardless of the costs to dominate our youth sports landscape. More than anything we need to bring youth sports back into perspective as a "training camp" for life. Where this may not be a realistic philosophy in an environment of adult big time sport, big money and big business entertainment, it is imperative for our youth. Teaching the intrinsic values of sport should be the number one goal and placing them on a pedestal above winning. Sport teaches invaluable lessons in the game of life. Learning how to prepare for success, developing an intense work ethic, recognizing the importance of teamwork and last but not least learning not to quit when things get tough. These all are useful tools in the game of life.

All of these values were instrumental in me defeating a life threatening illness and I understand their worth all too well. Today, my experiences have led me to teach advanced dietary and exercise strategies geared at overweight adults and children.

Possible Solutions

It is easy to point out the problems, but what about finding solutions. Starting with our youth, educational prevention programs are important but are not a panacea. School districts are pondering drug testing, but can we afford the cost? In my home state of Pennsylvania they are implementing body mass index (BMI) ratings of all students in our battle against childhood obesity. Body mass index is kg/m2 and is a measurement of weight in ratio to height. One strategy would be to educate school nurses and officials on what might be the telltale signs of anabolic drug abuse in a radical change in BMI primarily in lean mass, along with other symptoms that may be red flags. These signals could be followed up with limited testing and then, if needed, medical evaluation and treatment. This would lessen the prohibitive costs of "across the board" drug testing while lessening the overall invasiveness of interdiction efforts. Recently, I spoke with my scientific mentor in this area, Dr. Charles Yesalis of Penn State. He mentioned how he would be willing, together with other experts, to draw up a "profiling" prototype to be used to teach school nurses and medical officials as a preliminary evaluation tool. This could help school medical officials identify potential students at risk and funnel them to appropriate medical attention or discipline. This would be a way to use an existing medical evaluation in our fight against obesity to help contain another issue of risky adolescent behavior.

Philosophically, I have never been a huge believer in "big government" being over-involved in private business or "invasive testing." However, used judiciously for the right reasons as a safety net for a public health issue involving children I believe such government actions are both appropriate and required for the general public's best interests. I would strongly suggest the adoption of a national school steroid policy combined with preventative legislation prohibiting non-medical genetic engineering and gene doping.

Obviously, funding for research for both long-term health effects and to improve drug detection technology are a basic need in strategies of containment or eradication. I would support the idea that the athletic federations themselves should assist in financially helping to clean their own mess. Ultimately, the reality facing us is that how we now proceed will determine the sports/social environment of our future. Are we willing to embrace these challenges? How much do we care about preserving the joy of sport for our youth, and what is the price of business?

> *"I believe we should have a serious discussion about legalizing steroid use for professional athletes and any other adults who, under a doctor's care, seek to improve their athletic performance."*

Performance-Enhancing Drugs Should Not Be Banned from Sports

Joan Ryan

In the following viewpoint, Joan Ryan contends that the public's reaction to athletes' use of steroids to improve their performance is overblown. Ryan asserts that the hysteria over performance-enhancing drugs is a result of misinformation, that steroid use has not been proven to cause any life-threatening health problems, and that steroids should not be banned from professional sports without further examination. Joan Ryan is a syndicated news columnist for the San Francisco Chronicle *and author of* Shooting from the Outside: How a Coach and Her Olympic Team Transformed Women's Basketball.

As you read, consider the following questions:

1. Professional baseball player Jason Giambi developed a pituitary tumor. Is that a known side effect of steroid use, according to Joan Ryan?

2. What has more risk, use of painkillers or steroids, according to the author?

3. Does Joan Ryan believe that a level playing field could be attained if steroids were banned from sports?

I believe we should have a serious discussion about legalizing steroid use for professional athletes and any other adults who, under a doctor's care, seek to improve their athletic performance.

But because steroid use without a prescription is not legal—and even with a prescription, against the rules of baseball and most other sports—the price Barry Bonds, Jason Giambi [professional baseball players] and others implicated in the BALCO [Bay Area Laboratory Co-Operative, the supplement company that supplied steroids to athletes] case are paying is a real one. Athletes who take steroids have no one to blame but themselves because they know what the fallout will be if they are discovered.

Why Such an Unfavorable Reaction?

For athletes caught up in the BALCO scandal, their characters have been impugned, their accomplishments denigrated. There have been screaming headlines, righteous trashing on the talk shows and, come spring, there surely will be boos and catcalls in every ballpark across North America.

But here's the question not being asked: Why is this the response to the revelations? Why is there such reefer-madness hysteria about steroids? The use of performance-enhancing drugs in sports is considered so abhorrent that, in the midst of war last January [2004], President [George W.] Bush highlighted its evils in his State of the Union address. And the U.S.

Stretch the Limits

It's important to note that what we consider perfectly natural and acceptable today was quite out of the ordinary not so long ago. 100 years ago, life expectancy in the U.S. was 50 years of age. Today it's 78. Thanks to technology, medicine, and pharmaceuticals we are today taller, stronger, faster, healthier, and can expect to live longer than ever before. Genetically enhanced agriculture, anti-aging technology, and other advancements we've yet to see today—all of which seem as foreign to us now as penicillin likely seemed 50 years ago—will push our longevity even higher. . . .

Sports is about exploring and stretching the limits of human potential. Going back even to the pre-modern Olympics, when athletes ate live bees and ate crushed sheep testicles to get a leg up on the competition, sports has never been some wholesome display of physical ability alone. Ingenuity, innovation, and knowledge about *what* makes us faster and stronger (and avoiding what might do more harm than good) has always been a part of the game.

Radley Balko, "Should We Allow Performance Enhancing Drugs in Sports?" Reason, January 23, 2008.

Congress has threatened to take time from military budgets and intelligence reform to crack down on steroids in professional baseball if the owners and union fail to do so.

Norm Fost, pediatrics professor and medical-ethics expert at the University of Wisconsin Medical School, is confounded by the paroxysms over steroids in sports.

"There's mass hysteria because of sheer misinformation," he says.

Are Steroids Truly Life-threatening?

He has been studying and writing about steroids in sports for more than 20 years. He has yet to find research that conclusively attributes a single death to steroid use. Former Raiders [Oakland, California football team] player Lyle Alzado believed steroids caused the brain tumor that eventually killed him, but there is no medical evidence to back up his claim—or any claim that steroid use causes cancer.

Former Tampa Bay Buccaneers player Steve Courson believed steroids caused his heart degeneration. But by his own admission, he took steroids in such large quantities over such a long period of time, and in combination with other drugs, that his heart failure likely was caused by the extraordinary abuse of the drug rather than the drug itself. Ingesting massive quantities of almost any drug, even over-the-counter painkillers, can cause serious damage.

A teenager's suicide in Texas was also blamed on steroids, prompting his father to mount a national campaign. Again, there is no conclusive evidence of a connection.

"How many teenagers commit suicide every year? Lots. And how many took steroids the day before? How many more drank Cokes or ate Big Macs?" Fost says.

The life-threatening health risks most of us have accepted as fact are anecdotal and largely speculative. (In last Sunday's [December 5, 2004] column, I wrote that Giambi's pituitary tumor was a known side effect of steroids. I since have learned it is not.) This isn't to say taking steroids or other performance-enhancing substances is risk-free. All drugs carry risk, which is why they should be prescribed and managed by a doctor, rather than a muscle-man peddling them out of the trunk of his car.

In truth, a football player is more likely to suffer permanent disability by simply playing the game than by taking steroids. There is more risk in taking painkillers and cortisone shots to play while injured—a common practice in football—

than in using steroids. Yet we allow adults to decide for themselves whether to throw their bodies in front of charging 350-pound linemen or pop pills to hurry back out on the field. Why are we so paternalistic about steroids?

Is a Level Playing Field Possible?

Critics might answer this way: Even if steroids were made legal, they would give athletes willing to take them an unfair advantage over those who are unwilling, thus undermining the imperative of a level playing field. The fact is the level playing field is a myth and always has been.

Some athletes and teams have always had advantages over others, whether in funding, equipment, access to nutrition, training methods, coaching, even ease of transportation. Yet somehow, great athletes still manage to emerge as winners despite the inequities—the Kenyan long-distance runners, for example.

"If baseball is so concerned about level playing fields, then why is George Steinbrenner's (New York Yankees) payroll six times bigger than my Milwaukee Brewers'?" Fost asks.

He remembers watching the 1988 Olympics on television. While Canadian sprinter Ben Johnson was fleeing in disgrace after testing positive for steroids, U.S. gold-medal swimmer Janet Evans was regaling a news conference with details about a new kind of swimsuit that had helped her cut through the water faster. It was a technological breakthrough, she noted, that had been kept secret from the East Germans, the Americans' swimming rivals.

Yet no one accused Evans or the U.S. of undermining the level playing field, much less cheating.

"The hypocrisy is remarkable." Fost says.

How Are Youth Affected?

And no more so than in Major League Baseball's argument that steroids must be eradicated because the sport needs to serve as a healthy example for the young folks. If baseball gives its stamp of approval to steroids, the thinking goes, then teenagers will think it's OK for them to use them, too.

One wonders, then, about all the beer ads at baseball parks. What kind of message does baseball's celebration of beer send to teenagers? Unlike steroids, alcohol kills 75,000 people a year in the United States.

"Not only are players not screened for alcohol, it's embraced and advertised," Fost says. "Baseball is delighted to be in cahoots with the alcohol industry."

The recent steroids stories are big news because baseball's greatest player has been branded a cheater. But he is considered a cheater in large part because we have turned steroids into some evil potion that threatens to destroy not only sports, but, if President Bush is to be believed, the well-being and moral fiber of our youth. I wonder how he and others reconcile this viewpoint with their admiration for Arnold Schwarzenegger, whose chemically created body launched the storied career that has landed him in the California governor's office.

I lean toward allowing steroids in professional sports. I understand why others disagree and am braced for the deluge of contrary e-mails. But in making the decision to ban steroids, baseball and other sports at least ought to take a few deep breaths and examine the issue with some clarity and neutrality, recognizing steroids as the pharmaceuticals they are, not the wicked plague of immorality they have come to represent.

> *"'We've all seen the statistics and read the articles about the impact steroids have on kids. This is a growing health threat.'"*

Young Athletes Use Steroids

Regan McMahon

In the following viewpoint, Regan McMahon maintains that young athletes are using performance-enhancing drugs, sometimes on recommendation from their coaches. McMahon describes the symptoms and health risks associated with steroid use, including severe emotional depression, which some experts believe can lead to suicide. Regan McMahon is the deputy book editor at the San Francisco Chronicle *and the author of* Revolution in the Bleachers: How Parents Can Take Back Family Life in a World Gone Crazy over Youth Sports.

As you read, consider the following questions:

1. Does steroid use lead to a quicker or slower than normal recovery time from injury, according to Regan McMahon?

2. Describe what the term "'roid rage" refers to, according to the author.

Regan McMahon, *Revolution in the Bleachers: How Parents Can Take Back Family Life in a World Gone Crazy over Youth Sports*. New York, NY: Gotham Books, 2007. Copyright © 2007 by Regan McMahon. Foreword copyright © 2007 by Bill Walton. All rights reserved. Used by permission of Penguin Group (USA) Inc.

3. According to McMahon, can steroids be taken in pill form, or only injected?

According to the Centers for Disease Control and Prevention, as many as 1.1 million young people 12 to 17 years old have used performance enhancing drugs (PEDs) or sports supplements, and steroid use—or "juicing"—among high school students more than doubled between 1991 and 2003. Statistics from the National Institute on Drug Abuse reveal that 3.4 percent of U.S. high school seniors admitted using steroids in 2005. And who knows how many kids surveyed didn't admit their usage?

"Depending on which national studies you read, estimates of usage among kids in 8th through 12th grade ranges between 4 and 11 percent," says Mark Fainaru-Wada, *San Francisco Chronicle* reporter and co-author with Lance Williams of *Game of Shadows: Barry Bonds, BALCO, and the Steroids Scandal That Rocked Professional Sports.*

Fainaru-Wada wrote a story for the *Chronicle* about Rob Garibaldi, a young baseball player in Petaluma, California, who was encouraged at 16 to use legal weight-gaining supplements by his high school coach, who was also a supplement salesman, and by 18 he was using steroids he procured in Mexico. His parents and psychiatrist say it was use of those drugs, and the resulting depression, rage and delusional behavior he suffered from, that led him to commit suicide at 24, in 2002, by shooting himself with a .357 Magnum he had stolen the day before. Garibaldi's father, Ray, told Fainaru-Wada he had confronted Rob a month earlier, demanding to know what drugs he was on. Rob erupted and started choking him, screaming, "I'm on steroids, what do you think? Who do you think I am? I'm a baseball player, baseball players take steroids. How do you think Bonds hits all his home runs? How do you think all these guys do all this stuff? You think they do it from just working out normal?"

Weight training and conditioning are part of high school sports programs, and anabolic steroids allow for significantly quicker recovery time from workouts and injuries, so more stress can be put on muscles in a smaller amount of time. A steroid abuser generally can work on the same group of muscles every day without needing any time for them to recover. So the athlete will get much larger than a nonuser during the same period of time.

Symptoms of steroid use include dramatic gains in size and strength, cysts, oily hair and skin and changes in behavior including paranoid jealousy, delusions, increased irritability and aggression, often referred to as 'roid rage. Steroids can also cause male-pattern baldness and shrunken testicles.

According to the American College of Sports Medicine, steroid use by adolescents has been linked to early heart disease, an increase in tendon injuries, liver tumors, testicular atrophy, severe acne and premature closure of growth plates.

Long-term health risks of steroids—which can be easily obtained on the Internet and injected or taken in pill form—include heart disease, stroke, kidney malfunction, liver disease, HIV risk, disfigurement, depression and premature death. When high school steroid use hits the evening news, it's often because an athlete who was juicing has committed suicide.

When a junior varsity baseball coach told Texas teen Taylor Hooton, an outgoing, popular athlete, that he needed to get bigger if he wanted to make the varsity baseball team at Plano West High School, he began using anabolic steroids and went from 175 pounds to 205 on his 6 foot 1 1/2 inch frame. He stopped taking them in May 2003 and slipped into a depression and, a month after his 17th birthday in July that year, committed suicide by hanging. "It's a pretty strong case that he was withdrawing from steroids and his suicide was directly related to that," Dr. Larry W. Gibbons, president and medical director of the Cooper Aerobics Center, a leading preventive medicine clinic in Dallas, told the *New York Times*. Taylor's fa-

Secret Code for Steroid Use

In our reporting, we've met young athletes and their kin, and they've told us there's a whole code that the coaches use in talking to the boys to tell them to use steroids. One phrase is: "You need to get bigger." Another is: "You need to get serious in the weight room." We talked to the mom of a Division I college baseball player, and he was told, "You need to take a trip to Mexico," a reference to where athletes can buy steroids cheaper. So by using phrases like that, the coaches can later say, "I never told him to use steroids."

It's hard for some teenage boys to gain weight. My son was pretty serious about weight training. He's a long, tall, lean guy. He's about 6 feet 2 inches and he lifted weights throughout his junior year in high school trying to gain some weight, and he also did some flaxseed oil and powdered supplements. And he only went from 162 to 165, despite fairly intense weight training and playing two other sports and eating all the time. It's just not that easy for some kids to gain weight. And when the coach says you need to get bigger, the way to get bigger is to use anabolic steroids, because that will help you put weight on—muscle on—right now.

Lance Williams, in an interview with
Regan McMahon for her book Revolution in the Bleachers,
New York: Gotham Books, 2007.

ther, Don Hooton, a director of worldwide marketing for Hewlett-Packard, founded the Taylor Hooton Foundation to fight steroid abuse and travels around the country speaking to high schools to build awareness of the dangers and prevalence of steroid use. "Don't tell me it's not a problem," Hooton told the *Times.* "My kid just died."

High schools are concerned about teen steroid use, but few have established testing practices. The tests are very expensive—costs can run as high as $250 each—and there is debate about how widespread steroid abuse is, how urgent the need for testing is, what appropriate punishment would be and who should mete it out, should a test come out positive. New Jersey was the first state to step in and mandate random testing of high school athletes participating in state championship events in the 2006–2007 academic year, a policy that would affect about 500 athletes. Anyone testing positive could be banned from competition for a year. When acting governor Richard J. Codey signed the executive order in December 2005, he estimated that 8 percent of New Jersey's 220,000 high school athletes—more than 17,000—were abusing steroids.

Codey told the *Associated Press*, "We've all seen the statistics and read the articles about the impact steroids have on kids. This is a growing health threat, one we can't leave up to individual parents, coaches or schools to handle."

> "The nationwide survey ... revealed a
> continued pattern of marked decline in
> youth steroids use and unwavering dis-
> approval of these performance-
> enhancing muscle builders."

Steroid Use Among Youth Is Declining

Marcia C. Smith

Marcia C. Smith, a columnist for the Orange County Register
*in California, maintains in the following viewpoint that today's
young people are steering clear of steroid use. Smith asserts that
because so many sports heroes, such as Olympic medal winners
and baseball all-stars, have been exposed and shamed for their
"drug cheating," the attitudes of most American students have
turned in favor of fair and drug-free competition.*

As you read, consider the following questions:

1. According to Marcia C. Smith, at one time were steroids
   frequently used by middle school and high school students?

2. What year did youth steroid use reach its peak, according to the author?

3. Does the George W. Bush administration want high schools to implement steroid testing programs?

America's kids have known what's going on. They have spent much of 2007 watching the sports world's doping dragnet catch cheaters, big and small.

They've witnessed American sports' kings and queens squirming beneath suspicions of anabolic steroids use and facing federal perjury charges for covering up their syringe-stuck success.

Fallen Heroes Provide Lessons

They've seen stars getting booed and humiliated and stripped of Olympic medals, a Tour de France leader's yellow jersey, a home-run record's untainted glory and their reputations as "clean" sportsmen.

When about 50 former and active players are expected to be revealed today [December 12, 2007] in George J. Mitchell's report on performance-enhancing drug use in major-league baseball, America's youth will get more characters to add to their already well cast cautionary tale about drug-cheating in sports.

There will be more names. More heroes to fall. More achievements to question. More shame on sports.

But there will also be more lessons for today's children—and tomorrow's professional athletes—to learn about fair, drug-free play.

Steroids Are Unpopular Among Youth

The government's gold standard of youth drug-use studies, the University of Michigan's Monitoring the Future study, shows that the years of doping crackdowns in major sports and heightened efforts for anti-drug education have had positive effects.

The nationwide survey of 48,025 students—not just athletes—revealed a continued pattern of marked decline in youth steroids use and unwavering disapproval of these performance-enhancing muscle builders.

Steroids never have been frequently used drugs among middle- and high schoolers. Their rate of usage, which hasn't crested far beyond 3 percent, ranks steroids higher than that of PCP and heroin but about half that of OxyContin and Vicodin.

Their epidemic status of steroids is non-existent compared with the 25–65 percent of surveyed students who have admitted to trying alcohol, inhalants, cigarettes or marijuana.

But it was the sharply declining rate of steroids use that became notable enough for President [George W.] Bush to mention in his Tuesday [December 11, 2007] press briefing. Even the White House's deputy drug czar Scott M. Burns held a conference call on youth steroids use this week.

"The message is out there now, loud and clear, every time an athlete gets caught . . . and has to face the negative consequences," said Burns, the nation's representative to the World Anti-Doping Agency. "It appears they (America's youth) are getting the message that those who participate in sports have to do so cleanly."

The study showed that 33 percent fewer students in 2007 (0.6 percent) acknowledged having used steroids in the past month than those who did in 2001 (0.9 percent).

Declining trends have become most noticeable after youth steroids use reached its peak around 2001, the same year when baseball's home-run numbers boomed and slugger Barry Bonds hammered a single-season-record 73 home runs beneath a suspicious cloud of performance-enhancing drug use.

Since 2001, the prevalence of surveyed students who have used steroids in their lifetime has decreased from 3 percent to 1.8 percent—a 40 percent drop. The prevalence of students who have used steroids in the past year has shrunk from 2 percent to 1.1 percent—a 45 percent drop.

Disapproval of steroids use remains high, hovering around 90 percent among 12th graders. This attitude against steroids coupled with continued drug testing might be the vaccine shot in the arm the sports world will need for drug-free future.

Society Is Turning Away from Steroid Use

"We're hopeful that steroids use (in society) is on a downturn for good," said Burns, the deputy director for state, local and tribal affairs at the White House Office of National Drug Control Policy. "This bodes well for the future."

Burns called the decline dramatic and the most significant since the downturn in youth drug use after the cocaine-related death of NBA [National Basketball Association] player Len Bias.

Other studies show similarly low usage rates for steroids. The Center for Disease Control's 2005 Youth Risk Surveillance System found that 4 percent of 13,953 high school students admitted using steroids. The youth sports non-profit LA84 Foundation reported that 1 percent of the 252 Southern California high school athletes acknowledged taking steroids.

Burns said the Bush Administration is pushing for more states to adopt steroids testing programs at the high school level and for major pro sports leagues to expand year-round, no-notice testing on a wider menu of performance-enhancing drugs.

Burns sounded convinced that today's younger generation has learned not to use steroids by seeing case after case unfold and sports star after sports star tumble.

He dropped a few names—track and field darling Marion Jones, sprinter Kelli White, cyclist Floyd Landis and sluggers Bonds and Mark McGwire, among others—as examples of celebrated athletes who have struggled after being suspected as cheats. As youngsters, it's easy to know right from wrong about steroids when you're not an adult athlete having to make a career-sustaining choice. The tough part might come when today's more enlightened generation has to keep tomorrow's sports fair and free of whatever magic pill comes after steroids.

| *"Tighten the testing and educate the young people on the dangers of steroids."*

Testing Student Athletes for Drugs Is Appropriate

B.J. Rains

In the following viewpoint, B.J. Rains describes the extensive use of steroids among major league baseball players and the resulting health problems. Rains maintains that steroid use has filtered down from the professional level to the collegiate level, and is becoming more frequent among youth. He further contends that because steroids are so harmful, increased drug testing of student athletes is necessary to prevent more unnecessary injuries. B.J. Rains, was a journalism student at Kansas University, and a reporter for the University Daily Kansan *when this article was published in 2005.*

As you read, consider the following questions:

1. What is one reason athletes use steroids, according to one Kansas University baseball player?
2. Is it difficult for athletes to obtain steroids, according to the author?

3. Does B.J. Rains believe that young people are informed about the risks involved with steroid use?

During the last few months [2005], one word has become associated with Major League Baseball. The word isn't hit, home run, strikeout or bunt. It actually has nothing to do with the game itself. That word? Steroids.

Baseball has gone under the microscope lately, as allegations of steroid use have surfaced. Retired big-name players such as Ken Caminiti and Jose Conseco have admitted to using steroids to get bigger and stronger. Both players won MVP [most valuable player] awards, and both admitted to taking steroids during their MVP seasons.

The Dangers of Steroid Use Exposed

Congress decided recently to hold hearings to discuss the use of steroids in baseball. Several current and former players testified. Until two seasons ago, Major League Baseball did not even test for steroids.

Why is everyone making a big deal about the use of steroids in baseball? Because using steroids is dangerous. Though steroids may help players bulk up, players are often in terrible health when they retire. Caminiti died last year [2004] at 41. An autopsy report found steroids to be a contributing factor. In an interview with *Sports Illustrated*, Caminiti admitted to using steroids and blamed them for the series of injuries he suffered.

"I'm still paying for it," Caminiti said to *Sports Illustrated*. "My tendons and ligaments got all torn up. My muscles got too strong for my tendons and ligaments. And now my body's not producing testosterone. You know what that's like? You get lethargic. You get depressed. It's terrible."

Steroid Use Among College Athletes

It also seems that steroids are present at the college level as well.

Possible Health Consequences of Anabolic Steroid Abuse

Hormonal System: Men

Infertility, breast development, shrinking of the testicles, and male-pattern baldness.

Hormonal System: Women

Enlargement of the clitoris, excessive growth of body hair, and male-pattern baldness.

Musculoskeletal System

Short stature (if taken by adolescents), and tendon rupture.

Cardiovascular System

Increases in LDL, decreases in HDL, high blood pressure, heart attacks, and enlargement of the heart's left ventricle.

Liver

Cancer and tumors.

Skin

Severe acne and cysts, oily scalp, jaundice, and fluid retention.

Infection

HIV/AIDS and hepatitis.

Psychiatric Effects

Rage, aggression, mania, and delusions.

National Institute on Drug Abuse,
"Research Report Series—Anabolic Steroid Abuse".
http://www.nida.nih.gov/ResearchReports/
steroids/AnabolicSteroids4.html.

After talking with a member of the KU [Kansas University] baseball team who asked to remain anonymous, I found out that steroid use was becoming more and more prominent at the collegiate level.

"I have played with and against players who have taken steroids," the player said. "I have not witnessed anyone take steroids, but guys have told me that they are doing it. I can notice a physical difference. They are bigger and stronger. It's an obvious difference."

The player said that athletes used steroids when they were stuck at a plateau and couldn't move up.

For example, if a player is stuck in the minor leagues and can't get past double-A, he might use steroids to give him that needed push toward the majors.

"I have not needed to take steroids, because I have had success at this level," the player said. "If I got to a point, where I was stuck at a certain level, and couldn't get any better, I would definitely consider taking them because they could help me get to the next level."

Steroid use is so prominent in college athletics that this player said he could obtain steroids with ease if he wanted to do so.

"If I wanted to take steroids, I know who I could call to get them," he said.

The NCAA [National Collegiate Athletic Association] currently tests players for steroids, but it is obviously not enough. The player said he was a member of a random NCAA steroids test, as well as a University-wide test. No Kansas players take steroids, he said. They are not tested in the offseason, however, which is when most of the players use steroids because they are able to get away with it.

Players take steroids to get bigger and stronger so they can make the Major Leagues. They want to make millions of dollars, and they weigh the risk of serious injury as less important than the risk of injury.

The Value of Steroid Testing

A study done by the National Youth Sports Research and Development Center in the fall of 2002 examined the use of steroids among American youth. Of the 1,553 youth athletes surveyed, approximately 1 percent of 10- to 14-year-old participants were using or had used anabolic steroids.

We need stricter steroids testing. The testing needs to be done in the offseason. Also, more tests need to be done throughout the year. The NCAA needs to scare these players from trying to sneak around the law and use these steroids. If we can eliminate steroid use in college, we can begin to eliminate steroid use in the professional ranks. Also, we need to inform our athletes about the dangers of steroids.

The study done by the National Youth Sports Research and Development Center showed that young athletes were not properly educated on the dangers of steroids.

More than a quarter of youth sports participants have received their knowledge of anabolic steroids from magazines or books, the study said.

If we plan on decreasing steroid use in the professionals, it starts with American youth. Tighten the testing and educate the young people on the dangers of steroids. Not only will it repair the integrity of America's sports, it will help decrease injuries and save people's lives. It's a win-win situation.

> "Student drug testing programs are unproven, invasive, expensive and, perhaps most important, potentially counterproductive."

Testing Student Athletes for Drugs Is Not Appropriate

Jennifer Kern

Jennifer Kern asserts in the following viewpoint that student drug testing programs do not reliably reduce the use of drugs among student athletes and should, therefore, not be implemented in schools. Kern further maintains that coaches and educators should focus their efforts on comprehensive and honest drug education to deter students from using illegal drugs. Jennifer Kern is the Youth Policy manager for the Drug Policy Alliance and co-author of the booklet Making Sense of Student Drug Testing: Why Educators Are Saying No.

As you read, consider the following questions:

1. According to Jennifer Kern, is there an abundance of information regarding scientific research on student drug testing programs?

2. Do government officials agree with researchers that students react negatively to random drug tests?

3. What are the peak drug-taking hours for teens, according to Jennifer Kern?

The drug czar's [John Walters, director of National Drug Control Policy] staff is touring the country hosting summits designed to entice local educators to start drug testing their students—randomly and without cause. Today the road show comes home and [Washington] D.C. administrators, coaches and counselors will get the hard sell. While White House officials will attempt to describe the programs in benign terms, I urge educators to do their own research. Student drug testing programs are unproven, invasive, expensive and, perhaps most important, potentially counterproductive.

Unproven and Invasive

Random student drug testing programs are unproven. Educators will notice a conspicuous absence of information regarding scientific research at this [George W.] Bush Administration summit. In fact, the only national, peer-reviewed study ever conducted on the topic compared 94,000 students in almost 900 U.S. schools with and without a drug testing program and found virtually no difference in illegal drug use. Furthermore, last November [2007] researchers from Oregon Health and Science University [OHSU] published results from randomized experimental trials that concluded random drug and alcohol testing did not reliably reduce past month drug and alcohol use among student athletes.

Drug testing is invasive and the collection of a specimen can be especially alienating to adolescents. With the looming specter of false positives, schools must ask students to disclose private health information regarding their prescription medications, raising additional anxieties—among students and faculty alike—about the potential for breaches in confidentiality and false accusations.

Random Drug Testing Does Not Deter Drug Use

Percentage of 12th Graders who Reported Using an Illicit Drug (other than marijuana) in the 2003 University of Michigan Drug Testing Study

Percentage of 12th Graders who Reported Using Marijuana in the 2003 University of Michigan Drug Testing Study

Illicit Drug Use Among 12th Graders in Schools with & without Drug Testing

Marijuana Use Among 12th Graders in Schools with & without Drug Testing

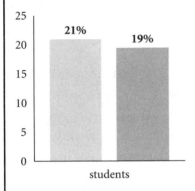

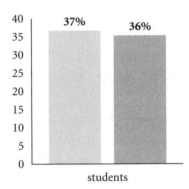

Schools with Student Drug Testing

Schools without Student Drug Testing

TAKEN FROM: Ryoko Yamaguchi, Lloyd D. Johnston, and Patrick M. O'Malley, "Relationship Between Student Illicit Drug Use and School Drug Testing Policies," *Journal of School Health*, April 2003.

Expensive and Counterproductive

For its high price tag, testing is inefficient in detecting drug problems. Though it may provide a false sense of security among school officials and parents, testing detects only a tiny fraction of users and misses too many who might be in real trouble. The Dublin School District in Ohio abandoned its $35,000 drug-testing program and instead hired two full-time substance abuse counselors.

Random drug testing programs are counterproductive. White House officials claim the students embrace the random searches, but strong evidence disputes their claims. The researchers from OHSU found attitudinal changes among students in schools with drug testing programs that indicate new risk factors for future substance use. Student athletes in schools with drug testing reported less positive attitudes toward school, less faith in the benefits of drug testing and less belief that testing was a reason not to use drugs, among other indicators. Those findings support objections that suspicion-less testing can erode relationships of trust between students and adults at school, damaging an essential component of a safe and rewarding learning environment.

Many other potential unintended consequences of random student drug testing programs become apparent upon closer inspection. While summit presenters insist the programs are non-punitive, they in fact rely on the threat of removing students from the very activities proven most effective in keeping them supervised and connected from 3:00 to 6:00 p.m.—peak drug taking hours for teens. If that's not punishment, what is?

Testing may also trigger oppositional behavior, such as trying to "beat" the test. The American Academy of Pediatrics warns that mandatory testing may inadvertently encourage more students to abuse alcohol—not included in many standard testing panels—or may motivate some drug-involved adolescents to switch to harder drugs that leave the system more quickly.

Oversimplified

We would better serve young people by facing the reality that there is no quick fix for the complex issues surrounding substance abuse. Much like the "Just Say No" approach, random drug testing oversimplifies the complexities of life faced by teenagers these days.

Instead of investing in surveillance, we should spend our time and resources educating students through comprehensive, interactive and honest drug education with assistance and support for students whose lives have been disrupted by substance use.

> "*Who in their infinite wisdom, with more girls participating in high school sports today, [thinks] that we don't have female athletes trying steroids?*"

Male Student Athletes Are Drug Tested More Often than Females

David Murphy

In the following viewpoint, St Petersburg Times staff writer David Murphy contends that the drug testing programs that many schools are implementing to detect the use of performance-enhancing drugs are bypassing female athletes. In discussing Florida's legislation that calls for random drug testing of athletes in male-dominated sports, Murphy questions the legality and wisdom of excluding women at a time when increasing numbers of females are participating in competitive sports.

As you read, consider the following questions:

1. Prevention program coordinator Jamie Blosser believes males and females use steroids for different reasons. In her opinion, what is the reason females tend to use steroids?

2. The Florida House Bill 461 aims to randomly test athletes who participate in what three sports?

3. The Centers for Disease Control and Prevention (CDC) collected data in 2005 that showed what percentage of high school girls in Hillsborough County, Florida, had tried steroids?

As a former Division I athlete and current prevention program coordinator at a substance abuse treatment center, Jamie Blosser is in a good position to offer perspective on the use of performance-enhancing drugs in sports. While the former Boston College rower and high school softball and tennis player said she has never witnessed a fellow female athlete use illegal steroids, she said it is happening more than most people would think.

"There's definitely similar pressure there in female sports," said Blosser, who works at the Hanley Center in West Palm Beach. "Girls and guys tend to use steroids for different reasons. Guys to build up muscles, girls to shed the fat and slim out their bodies and put on lean muscles. Guys want to build up, girls want to slim down. . . . Between the media images that girls and guys are exposed to now, that's certainly an added pressure."

Testing Only Males Questioned

That makes some administrators and coaches, not to mention legal experts, wonder why the high school steroid-testing program passed by the [Florida] state Legislature last month targets only athletes in predominantly male sports.

House Bill 461, expected to be signed into law Tuesday [June 2007], calls for the random testing of up to one percent of all athletes in three sports: football, baseball and weightlifting. According to data collected by the Florida High School Athletic Association [FHSAA], 94 percent of athletes who participated in those sports during the 2005–06 school year were

How to Spot Girls' Steroids Abuse

- Sudden weight gain of 20 or 30 pounds of muscle, rather than fat, and greater muscle strength.

- Increase in facial and body hair, and loss of hair on the head.

- Deepening of the voice, a decrease in menstrual cycles and stunted growth, including smaller breasts.

- Sudden development of severe acne on the face and back.

- Increased appetite.

- Blood clots.

- Aggressive behavior or angry outbursts, known as "roid rage."

- Paranoia, hallucinations and psychotic behavior.

- Development of liver abnormalities and tumors.

- Elevated blood cholesterol and triglyceride levels, indicating premature onset of hardening of the arteries.

USATODAY.com,
"Girls Are Abusing Steroids Too—
Often to Get That Toned Look," April 26, 2005.
http://www.usatoday.com/news/health/
2005-04-25-girls-steroids_x.htm.

boys. A 2005 survey conducted by the Centers for Disease Control and Prevention [CDC] estimated that 2.8 percent of high school girls in the state had tried illegal steroid pills or injections at least once in their lives compared with 5.0 percent of boys.

Michael Stutzke, who helped implement one of the first drug-testing programs in the state [Florida] at Sebastian River High in 1996, said he thinks it is a mistake to exclude girls from testing.

"I happen to be a very big supporter of Title IX, and I believe if we are going to test guys, we should test girls," the longtime athletic director said. "Who in their infinite wisdom, with more girls participating in high school sports today, (thinks) that we don't have female athletes trying steroids?"

Student Drug Testing Deemed Legal

In many ways, the program the FHSAA hopes to implement for the upcoming school year can be traced to a small logging community in northwestern Oregon that prides itself on peace and solitude.

In the early 1990s, Vernonia, Ore., was the site of a landmark battle in the war on drugs (and, it turns out, the war on drug testing) as the family of a seventh-grade athlete challenged the random drug-testing program the local school district had installed two years earlier.

The Supreme Court ultimately ruled in favor of the school district, largely because of athletes' lower expectations of privacy (they shower together) and the need to protect their safety.

Subsequent court rulings have affirmed and expanded the Supreme Court's decision in the Vernonia case, and school districts across the country have had little legal trouble testing their athletes. Stutzke, for example, followed the Vernonia court case closely and used it as justification for starting the program at Sebastian River.

Gender Bias a Concern

But the Florida legislation, as it currently reads, could open the door for a different type of legal challenge.

Rep. Marcelo Llorente, the Miami Republican who has pushed for steroid testing for four years, said he is convinced the program is constitutional. Llorente said the legislation singles out baseball, football and weightlifting because of their reliance on strength and the logical correlation between those activities and the potential benefits of steroids.

Still, FHSAA commissioner John Stewart said he has some legal concerns, and the association likely will have to test athletes in sports such as softball and flag football.

"Quite frankly, we are going to talk to Rep. Llorente," Stewart said. "I think a female counterpart will have to be used to keep it out of the courts."

Perry A. Zirkel, a national expert on education law at Lehigh University in Bethlehem, Pa., said the possibility of a discrimination lawsuit does exist, though he said the state could argue it was singling out sports, not genders. If girl weightlifters were tested along with boy weightlifters, he estimated the chances of a plaintiff winning a discrimination suit at just 1 in 10. If the FHSAA tested only male weightlifters, he said the chances of winning would jump to about 8 in 10.

"Frankly, if I were in the legislature, I think what I would try to do, if I was convinced this was a bill that was important, I would make sure that it was applied gender blind," Zirkel said. "If you are going to do weightlifting, do girls weightlifting. Or maybe even add some other sports."

Because the state has said it will represent the FHSAA in any legal challenges stemming from the testing program, the association does not have to worry about funding costly court cases.

Nevertheless, the survey data collected by the CDC for its Youth Risk Behavior Survey in 2005 bears a stark warning, particularly for local administrators. One of the Florida areas surveyed was Hillsborough County. And 3.5 percent of high school girls here said they had tried steroids at least once.

Periodical Bibliography

The following articles have been selected to supplement the diverse views presented in this chapter.

Shaun Assael   "High School Drug Testing in New Jersey—Is it Worth It?" *ESPN the Magazine*, December 14, 2007.

Radley Balko   "Should We Allow Performance Enhancing Drugs in Sports? One Argument in Favor," *Reason*, January 23, 2008.

Jason Blevins   "Schools Say Yes to Drug Testing: Parents Want the Random Checks, but Opponents Say the Practice Is Useless," *The Denver Post*, May 18, 2008.

Joy Goodwin   "Nowhere to Run," *Elle*, August 2008.

Sanjay Gupta   "The Truth About Steroids and Sports," CBS News.com, February 3, 2008.

Scott Lafee   "The Race Against Gene Doping," *San Diego Union-Tribune*, July 27, 2008.

Maureen O'Hagan   "Random Student Drug Tests Banned," *Seattle Times*, March 14, 2008.

Rebecca Shore   "How We Got Here: A Timeline of Performance-Enhancing Drugs in Sports," *Sports Illustrated*, March 11, 2008.

Jacqueline Stenson   "Kids on Steroids Willing to Risk It All for Success: Users Say They'd Take Drugs to Excel Even If It Shortened Their Lives," MSNBC.com, March 3, 2008.

Mark Zeigler   "Doping Specter Looms Over World's Best Athletes," *San Diego Union-Tribune*, August 8, 2008.

For Further Discussion

Chapter 1

1. Some of the viewpoints in this chapter discuss the influence that parents and coaches can have on youth sports. Based on what you have read, do you think adults have a positive or negative effect on young athletes? Explain your answer.

2. Christian Malone and Jeffrey Standen write about whether athletes should be role models for young people. Do you believe it is fair to expect athletes to be role models in all aspects of life? Why or why not?

3. Brady Delander writes that children with disabilities receive tremendous physical and emotional benefits from participating in sports. From your reading, what suggestions could you offer an individual with disabilities who is hesitant to try a particular sport?

Chapter 2

1. Doug Jolley maintains that the Academic Performance Rate (APR) implemented by the National Collegiate Athletic Association (NCAA) will help ensure that student athletes receive an adequate academic education while in school. Elia Powers argues that the APR will lead to an increase in academic fraud. Do you think the APR is a successful tool? Why or why not?

2. Al Woods argues that college athletes should be paid a salary, while Krikor Meshefejian maintains that receiving a college scholarship is enough payment. Which argument do you find more convincing? Explain your answer.

3. Some of the authors in this chapter discuss the college athletic recruiting process. Are there issues in the recruiting process that you believe should be reformed? Explain your answer.

Chapter 3

1. Luke Kohler contends that fulfilling racial and gender equality in sports is not as important as hiring the most qualified people. Do you agree? Why or why not?

2. Some of the viewpoints in this chapter discuss the effect Title IX has had and is having on men's athletic programs. Do you believe Title IX is fair to both men and women athletes? Explain your answer.

3. Regan McMahon asserts that the prevalence of elite sports clubs is one of the main problems of today's youth sports culture. Based on your reading, how are these elite clubs affecting youth sports? Do you agree that they have a detrimental impact? Why or why not?

Chapter 4

1. Steve Courson maintains that performance-enhancing drugs are dangerous and should be banned from sports. Joan Ryan argues that performance-enhancing drugs should be examined more thoroughly before totally prohibiting their use. Which argument do you find most persuasive? Explain your answer.

2. According to Regan McMahon, many young athletes are using performance-enhancing drugs, while Marcia C. Smith maintains that most students disapprove of steroid use and that the rate of usage among young people has dramatically declined. Do you believe steroid use is prevalent among student athletes? Explain your reasoning.

3. B.J. Rains argues that steroid testing of student athletes should be increased, given the serious health risks involved with steroid usage. Jennifer Kern maintains that student drug testing programs are invasive, alienating, and counterproductive. Which argument do you agree with? Why?

4. David Murphy writes that school drug testing programs are bypassing female athletes. Do you think steroid use among female athletes is as prevalent as use among male athletes? Do you believe that males and females should be tested equally, regardless of the sport? Why or why not?

Organizations to Contact

The editors have compiled the following list of organizations concerned with the issues debated in this book. The descriptions are derived from materials provided by the organizations. All have publications or information available for interested readers. The list was compiled on the date of publication of the present volume; the information provided here may change. Readers need to remember that many organizations take several weeks or longer to respond to inquiries.

American Association of Adapted Sports Programs (AAASP)
945 Indian Creek Dr., Clarkston, GA   30021
(404) 294-0070 • fax: (404) 294-5788
e-mail: sports@adaptedsports.org
Web site: www.adaptedsports.org

The American Association of Adapted Sports Programs supports the concept that school-based sports are a vital part of the education process of students. The association has adapted sports, based on functional ability, for interscholastic athletic systems. The AAASP provides press releases, a video and photo gallery, and publishes the newsletter *The Adapted Sports Report*.

American College of Sports Medicine (ACSM)
401 W. Michigan St., Indianapolis, IN   46202-3233
(317) 637-9200 • fax: (317) 634-7817
Web site: www.acsm.org

The largest sports medicine and exercise science organization in the world, ACSM promotes healthy lifestyles and is committed to the diagnosis, treatment, and prevention of sports-related injuries and to the advancement of the science of exercise. ACSM publishes the monthly journal *Medicine & Science in Sports & Exercise* and the bimonthly *ACSM's Health & Fitness Journal* and *Current Sports Medicine Reports*.

Athletes for a Better World (ABW)
1740 Barnesdale Way NE, Atlanta, GA   30309
(404) 892-2328
Web site: www.abw.org

ABW advocates a "Code for Living" that encourages discipline, integrity, respect, cooperation, and compassion in sports environments. The organization provides free printed, educational materials and publishes a quarterly newsletter.

Center for the Study of Sport in Society
Northeastern University, Boston, MA   02115
(617) 373-4025 • fax: (617) 373-4566
e-mail: sportinsociety@neu.edu
Web site: www.sportinsociety.org

The Center's mission is to increase awareness of sport and its relation to society. It also develops programs that identify sports-related problems and offer solutions to these problems, as well as programs that promote the benefits of sport. The Center's programs include Disability in Sport and the Degree Completion Program. The Center provides research publications concerning such topics as diversity in sport and sport in society, as well as the annual *Racial Report Card*.

National Alliance for Youth Sports (NAYS)
2050 Vista Parkway, West Palm Beach, FL   33411
(561) 684-1141 • fax: (561) 684-2546
e-mail: nays@nays.org
Web site: www.nays.org

NAYS is a nonprofit organization that advocates for positive and safe sports and activities for youth. It offers programs and services for everyone involved in youth sports experiences, including professional administrators, volunteer administrators, volunteer coaches, officials, parents, and young athletes. It publishes the magazine *Sporting Kid* and its Web site provides links to numerous informative articles and books.

National Association for Girls and Women in Sport (NAGWS)

1900 Association Dr., Reston, VA 20191
(703) 476-3450
Web site: http://iweb.aahperd.org/nagws

NAGWS is a nonprofit organization of professional educators dedicated to achieving equality in sports for girls and women. It produces the online *Women in Sport and Physical Activity Journal* and the online newsletter *GWS News*.

National Association of Intercollegiate Athletics (NAIA)

1200 Grand Blvd., Kansas City, MO 64106-2304
(816) 595-8000 • fax: (816) 595-8200
Web site: http://naia.cstv.com

NAIA promotes the education and development of students through intercollegiate athletic participation. Member institutions, although diverse, share a common commitment to the principle that participation in athletics serves as an integral part of the total educational process. The association provides a hotline offering the latest college sports information, and publishes an online magazine *NAIA News*, as well as the *NAIA Presidential Perspective*.

National Collegiate Athletic Association (NCAA)

700 W. Washington St., Indianapolis, IN 46206-6222
(317) 917-6222 • fax: (317) 917-6888
Web site: www.ncaa.org

NCAA is the administrative body that oversees intercollegiate athletic programs. It publishes reports on student athlete graduation rates in colleges, transcripts from its annual conventions discussing academic and athletic rules, and special reports on sports programs, finances, and television. NCAA publications include *Gender Equity in Intercollegiate Athletics* and *A Career in Professional Athletics*.

Nicholas Institute of Sports Medicine and Athletic Trauma (NISMAT)

130 East 77th St., 10th Floor, New York, NY   10021
(212) 434-2700
e-mail: info@nismat.org
Web site: www.nismat.org

NISMAT is the first American hospital-based facility dedicated to the study of sports medicine. Its Web site offers information about nutrition, physical therapy, cardiology, training, orthopedics, and other hot topics. The institute also publishes research reports.

Positive Coaching Alliance (PCA)

1001 N. Rengstorff Ave., Suite 100
Mountain View, CA   94043
(866) 725-0024 • fax: (650) 969-1650
e-mail: pca@positivecoach.org
Web site: www.positivecoach.org

Established at Stanford University in 1998, the nonprofit PCA provides live, research-based training workshops and practical tools for coaches, parents, and leaders involved with youth sports programs to teach life lessons through positive coaching. The alliance offers a video, *Honoring the Game: A Vision of a Positive Youth Sports Culture*, and publishes the newsletter *Momentum*, as well as the monthly "Good Coaching Case Studies."

Women's Sports Foundation

Eisenhower Park, 1899 Hempstead Turnpike, Suite 400
East Meadow, NY   11554
(516) 542-4700 • fax: (516) 542-4716
e-mail: info@WomensSportsFoundation.org
Web site: www.womenssportsfoundation.org

Founded by professional tennis star Billie Jean King in 1974, the Women's Sports Foundation supports the participation of women in sports activities and seeks to educate the public about athletic opportunities for women. It publishes the quarterly newsletter, *The Woman's Sports Experience*, and has published several articles, including "Exercise and Fitness" and "Tips on Getting Girls Active."

Bibliography of Books

Marcia K. Anderson, Susan J. Hall, and Gail P. Parr — *Foundations of Athletic Training: Prevention, Assessment, and Management.* Philadelphia: Lippincott Williams & Wilkins, 2008.

Shaun Assael — *Steroid Nation: Juiced Home Run Totals, Anti-aging Miracles, and a Hercules in Every High School: The Secret History of America's True Drug Addiction.* New York: ESPN Books, 2007.

Karen Blumenthal — *Let Me Play: The Story of Title IX: The Law that Changed the Future of Girls in America.* New York: Atheneum Books, 2005.

William G. Bowen and Sarah A. Levin — *Reclaiming the Game: College Sports and Educational Values.* Princeton, NJ: Princeton University Press, 2003.

Adrian Burgos Jr. — *Playing America's Game: Baseball, Latinos, and the Color Line.* Berkeley, CA: University of California Press, 2007.

Karen P. Depauw and Susan J. Gavron — *Disability Sport.* Champaign, IL: Human Kinetics Publishers, 2005.

James J. Duderstadt — *Intercollegiate Athletics and the American University: A University President's Perspective.* Ann Arbor, MI: University of Michigan Press, 2003.

David Galehouse and Ray Lauenstein — *The Making of a Student Athlete.* Sunnyvale, CA: Advisor Press, 2004.

John R. Gerdy — *Air Ball: American Education's Failed Experiment with Elite Athletics.* Jackson, MS: University Press of Mississippi, 2006.

Richard D. Ginsburg, Stephen Durant, and Amy Baltzell — *Whose Game Is It Anyway?* New York: Houghton Mifflin, 2006.

Susan S. Klein — *Handbook for Achieving Gender Equity Through Education.* Mahwah, NJ: Lawrence Erlbaum, 2007.

Richard E. Lapchick — *New Game Plan for College Sport.* Westport, CT: Praeger Publishers, 2006.

Madeline Levine — *The Price of Privilege: How Parental Pressure and Material Advantage Are Creating a Generation of Disconnected and Unhappy Kids.* New York: HarperCollins, 2006.

Chris Lincoln — *Playing the Game: Inside Athletic Recruiting in the Ivy League.* Chicago: Nomad Press, 2004.

Kyle Maynard — *No Excuses.* Washington, DC: Regnery Publications, 2005.

Eileen McDonagh and Laura Pappano — *Playing with the Boys: Why Separate Is Not Equal in Sports.* New York: Oxford University Press, 2007.

Regan McMahon · *Revolution in the Bleachers: How Parents Can Take Back Family Life in a World Gone Crazy over Youth Sports.* New York: Gotham Books, 2007.

Brian L. Porto · *A New Season: Using Title IX to Reform College Sports.* Westport, CT: Praeger Publishers, 2003.

Shaun Powell · *Souled Out?: How Blacks Are Winning and Losing in Sports.* Champaign, IL: Human Kinetics Publishers, 2007.

Cal Ripken Jr. and Rick Wolff · *Parenting Young Athletes the Ripken Way: Ensuring the Best Experience for Your Kids in Any Sport.* New York: Gotham Books, 2006.

Jeff Rutstein · *The Steroid Deceit: A Body Worth Dying For?* Boston: Custom Fitness Publishing, 2006.

George Selleck · *Raising a Good Sport in an In-Your-Face World: Seven Steps to Building Character on the Field—and Off.* Chicago: Contemporary Books, 2003.

Michael Silver and Natalie Coughlin · *Golden Girl: How Natalie Coughlin Fought Back, Challenged Conventional Wisdom, and Became America's Olympic Champion.* Emmaus, PA: Rodale Books, 2006.

Michael Sokolove *Warrior Girls: Protecting Our Daughters Against the Injury Epidemic in Women's Sports.* New York: Simon & Schuster, 2008.

Bruce Svare *Crisis on Our Playing Fields: What Everyone Should Know About Our Out of Control Sports Culture and What We Can Do to Change It.* Delmar, NY: Sports Reform Press, 2004.

Jim Thompson *Positive Coaching in a Nutshell.* Palo Alto, CA: Warde Publishers, 2007.

Tanni Grey Thompson *Aim High.* Pembroke Dock, Wales: Accent Press, 2007.

Warren Willey *Better Than Steroids.* Victoria, British Columbia: Trafford Publishing, 2007.

Andrew Zimbalist *The Bottom Line: Observations and Arguments on the Sports Business.* Philadelphia: Temple University Press, 2006.

Index

DATE DUE

JAN 10 2011			